Night Moves
Twenty-four letters

Night Moves
Twenty-four letters

between
Dominic Lash
and
David R J Stent

Sticking Place Books
New York

This text is comprised of lightly edited versions of letters that were exchanged by email between May 2025 and January 2026. The format was inspired by *The Parkland Mysteries* by Jeff Dolven and Joshua Kotin (The Yellow Papers 6, Amsterdam, 2023).

The authors would like to thank the following for their help and support: Phil Baber, Paul Cronin, David Grundy, Kate Hendry, Sarah Hughes, Martine McDonagh, and Anat Pick.

www.stickingplacebooks.com

ISBN 979-8-89976-076-1

Letter one—David to Dominic

So, watching *Night Moves* for the first time, I blind-scribbled notes in the darkness. A lot of thoughts, memorable sequences and images, the specifics of which will no doubt come up again. It seems important to set out some basics. The 2013 film is directed by Kelly Reichardt, written by Reichardt and Jonathan Raymond. Three main characters: we first join the ambiguous partnership of twenty-something environmental activists Josh and Dena mid-stream, mid-plan—in fact, scoping the scene of a crime-to-come. We follow the duo as they purchase a boat and travel to the home of Harmon, our third (older) character known to Josh but not to Dena—the kind of imbalance of knowledge that takes on great weight as things progress… destabilising ripples. The boat (re-christened *Night Moves*) is transformed into a homemade bomb and, under cover of darkness, is piloted upriver in order to blow up a river dam, with the intention of shocking people into renewed awareness of the environmental damage such structures deliver and symbolise. As much as a thriller set in the world of environmental activism, the film sets out a study of idealism and hubris, perhaps even a wry takedown of the lack of cogency on the Left, raising questions about the efficacy and status of revolutionary action, and the moment at which violence becomes justified / inevitable / irresistible / desperate… It also delivers a grinding, tense depiction of rising fear, guilt, paranoia and complicity—through a narrative shape that builds up to unravel, as things slide out of control, at different speeds for different characters.

The performances are curiously sober, verging on staid at times (which weirdly reminded me of some of the acting in *Eyes Wide Shut*, Nicole Kidman especially delivering lines as if lulling. A. Dog. To. Sleep—

but at which I thrilled because I was convinced that Kubrick wanted a kind of *dream slur*...), emphasising, I suppose, a form of hardened conviction, blinkered surety... The uptight intensity of Josh is captured in Eisenberg's pinched silences: an actor, it seems to me, adept at giving off a fume of tacit judgement, mutely simmering with contempt for what he sees as stupidity (or lack of conviction) in others (see also his immature pucker in the more verbose, Sorkin-fed-motor-mouthed Zuckerberg), quick to anger, arrogant. Josh's refusal of frivolity recurs a few times early on, leaving any light-heartedness to Dena and Harmon, whose more obvious connection is already a blow to the world as he saw it (and his leadership role in it). The anxiety that Eisenberg can get into his voice feeds into an unstable portrayal of the 'deadly earnest', the pose that is no doubt requisite for the wannabe revolutionary as much as the true.

That said, the sense of purpose shared with Dena is palpable but strangely cold and clinical (even dissociated at times). Both are taciturn in the sense that, in the early scenes, all they think about (and, it is implied, have thought about for some time) is their plan and its unique and penetrating importance and effectiveness, as if it were the only act that might cut through for such a problem of global proportions. Their personal relationship is presented as undefined, deliberately soft-edged. It is not clear what kind of affection exists between them, whether they are (or have been) lovers, or if their bond is purely militant, ideological, all business.

Is this enough scene setting?

I did want to end by mentioning the scene where Josh and Dena, on their way to Harmon, stop their truck beside a roadkill deer, which Josh declares as both pregnant and still warm on the night-time tarmac.

One might say that the script here falls into a slightly clumsy framing of a moral quandary—a neat, nested metaphor for death and potential life, wild nature having been cut down by human activity yet with a chance of resurrection, etc.—but the scene did stick in my mind. As much as watching a sense of duty, responsibility, even compassion stir an otherwise impassive character for a moment—and there was a feeling that in another cinematic universe a steaming bloody fawn would be wrenched from the dead womb and heroically resuscitated—what I think we see (and I want to watch this scene again in particular) is half-hearted concern for the 'right thing' culminating in the decision to pull the mother and child off the tarmac and to let the body slip out of sight down a gravel siding. The horrific, prolonged sound of that descent was particularly disturbing. A loaded sidelining, echoing the film's concern for 'ends and means'. Sacrifices are made to focus on the task at hand.

Letter two

Dear David,

It's wonderful to get your reactions upon a first viewing, because one of the things that led me to suggest this film was precisely my changing experiences with it over repeated viewings. (Not that I want to claim any kind of expert grasp of it, but it might be worth saying that I have seen it quite a few times, and taught it to undergraduates once or twice as well.) I think you've grasped much more of it than I was able to on my first viewing! Another motivating factor for suggesting it was the fact that it gets much shorter shrift than it deserves, even from Reichardt enthusiasts. Even the regularly on-the-money Jonathan Rosenbaum describes it as "conventional and predictable", involving "all-too-familiar genre exercises" (although I do agree with him that the connection between this film and Arthur Penn's 1975 film of the same name is unclear, and perhaps unnecessarily distracting).[*]

But *is* the film "conventional" and "predictable"; is the way it works with genre "all-too-familiar"? Those seem to me precisely the kinds of question that the film wants us to ask. Which conventions are in play, and how? What kinds of predictions do we make as viewers? Which ones do we get right? Which ones does it not even occur to us to make? What's the relationship between predictions and assumptions in our understanding of narrative cinema? I rather get the sense that some of the negative reactions that the film received were due to taking it as some kind of initially promising—but then disappointingly fumbled—thriller, precisely of a more familiar stripe. Justin Chang missed the point exquisitely in *Variety* when he wrote that the film "might have been

---

[*]   See   https://jonathanrosenbaum.net/2025/03/crossing-kelly-reichardts-wilderness/.

close to perfect had it clocked in at a tight 80 minutes or so, rather than pushing on for another half-hour".* Whereas your description of it as creating "a narrative shape that builds up to unravel" seems exactly right—it all leads up to what seems to me to be one of the most remarkable endings of any film made this century, which (to get very much ahead of ourselves) is the culmination of a kind of claustrophobic agoraphobia that builds steadily throughout the second half of the film. Reichardt has said that they talked a lot about *Crime and Punishment* while making the film.

Night Moves is about consequences and aftermaths and the differences between them, as well as the difference between collectivity and togetherness. What's the difference between a collective action and doing some stuff at the same time and place as other people are doing some stuff? In what ways would and wouldn't we describe our three protagonists as *doing the same thing* in all their shenanigans with boats, fertilizer, detonators, and the like? I don't disagree about the wryness of its commentary on the left (something it shares with the use of Air America talk radio in *Old Joy*), but I also think its chief concerns are more to do with extremism than with any particular flavour of it. (As in, the film *could*—in a way—have been about right-wing terrorism.) Although putting it that way is very misleading, because it makes it sound like the film is in the business of making bland statements about how the far left blurs into the far right, which is precisely what it isn't doing. It's about acting for reasons. I really like your description of how all that the characters "think about (and, it is implied, have thought about for some time) is their plan". This is absolutely true, but what hits both Josh and Dena like a ton of bricks

<hr>

* https://variety.com/2013/film/global/night-moves-review-venice-toronto-1200593646/.

(but not, I think, Harmon, who literally disappears after the three go their separate ways, becoming merely a muffled voice on a mobile phone) is that in all this planning they'd given absolutely no thought to what would happen afterwards. This is obviously some kind of deficiency, but it doesn't mean that their plan wasn't a *plan*. Which all renders very richly complex the question of precisely what it means to make "sacrifices" so as to "focus on the task at hand". How do we describe what exactly "the task at hand" *is*? I would suggest that interrogating what it means to act according to a plan—or not to—is one of Reichardt's central interests; I've written about this with regard to *Certain Women* but I think it's an illuminating question to apply to all of Reichardt's films.*

We should probably match the actors to the parts: Jesse Eisenberg is Josh; Dakota Fanning is Dena; Peter Sarsgaard is Harmon. Reichardt's interest in getting very experienced, professional, and often well-known actors to underplay I find fascinating. I like your comparison with *Eyes Wide Shut* because it seems to me very precisely wrong! In the Kubrick, as you say, the style of performance is meant to prevent us from forgetting that we are watching performances—by Tom Cruise and Nicole Kidman. Whereas here, though of course we can appreciate the skill of the actors if we go looking for it, the performances we're meant to be paying attention to are not those by Eisenberg and Fanning, but by Josh and Dena. (Think of Josh's sullen refusal to contribute to the roleplay when the two of them buy the boat, his rather conspicuous lack of response to her "right, honey?") Peter Bradshaw has

---

* "'A fair curve from a noble plan': *Certain Women*" was originally published in *Movie: A Journal of Film Criticism* in 2020 (https://warwick.ac.uk/fac/arts/scapvc/film/movie/contents/movie_issue9_certainwomen.pdf). A somewhat revised version appears in *Haunting the World* (SUNY Press, 2025).

described the performances as "closed and opaque" which is both exactly right and exactly wrong. I think the *characters* are often closed and opaque; the skill of this style of performance is precisely how intelligible it can be, onscreen. There are plenty of ambiguities in the performances here, but they're not evasions. It matters whether we're dealing with absences or with secrets. (And while we're on the subject of ambiguities, you're right to flag up that it's not clear whether or not Josh and Dena "are (or have been) lovers"; either way, though, the question is very clearly relevant to Josh. Remember him sloping off when he hears Harmon and Dena having sex, as well as the appearance of what is surely a tinge of jealousy when he finds out that she's been persistently phoning Harmon, not him, after the explosion.)

You're right about the way the film raises the possibility of clumsy metaphor with the encounter with the dead deer. (I suppose it's out of the question that this is an allusion to magnificent "D'oh!" "A deer!" "A female deer!" sequence in "Bart Gets an Elephant"? It will be good, when the time comes, to consider the humour in this film, of which I think there's more than initially meets the eye.) But anyway, the question of description crops up again here: exactly what *is* the clumsy metaphor? Something to do with pregnancy, as in the familiar banalities about the "wish being father to the deed", which don't seem to me to say anything beyond the fact that we sometimes do what we want to do? (Though it may also be relevant that Shakespeare's Henry IV tells his son that, when he thought he would never hear his father speak again, his "wish was father... to that thought". This is something like an accusation of wishful thinking, but more complex.) One way of reading the metaphor here would be that the inevitability with which gravity pulls the dead deer with its unborn child down the slope allows Josh to tell himself that there was nothing else he could have done. Although all this is made more complicated by the fact that he didn't need to stop (Dena: "You're stopping?"), as well as that there may very well have been no other options available to him. He was going to euthanise the unborn deer? How exactly? Or, as you say, heroically rip a very possibly unviable faun from its mother's womb? A lot of what the film is interested in might be tied up in the realisation that doing something so that you can tell yourself there was nothing else you could have done is not, in and of itself, proof that there *was* another option available to you.

Maybe we should go back to the beginning now and try going through more or less scene-by-scene?

Letter three

Thanks, Dom, for these thoughts, which are fascinating. They make me aware of how green I am in terms of my knowledge of Reichardt's work, cast in relief by your sustained research and previous writing. Amusingly, I briefly had a sensation of being involved in a plan, the scope and shape of which I could only be partly aware of, combined with a feeling that I may always be catching up... Still, one hopes such an imbalance of knowledge will prove productive!

There is so much to think about in your letter it is difficult to know how to respond, but I will get to some thoughts about the opening scenes, which I agree is a good way of proceeding. But many of your comments contextualised my first viewing of the film, so it felt worth sticking with them for a moment. As you say, it will be intriguing to see how exactly we can unpick the film's relationship to patterns of convention, expectation, and prediction, related to genre, yes, but in wider senses too, not least the interplay of character and performance. Your mention of 'prediction' here seemed particularly interesting, both in relation to character interactions (or lack of them) and audience experience. I'm ambivalent about the complexities of thinking 'outside' films in the process of watching them—something that I am not particularly good at and which I consciously try to avoid doing most of the time, not wanting to predict any twist or anticipate any ending... perhaps keen to get lost in the story? I still do it, of course, and perhaps this ambivalence is a useful tip. It's potentially interesting to consider how the play of convention has also been fused into the characters we're watching—in the face of an apathetic response to the climate crisis, what is needed is an action (movie)... arguably one way to look at the "slick" renaming of the boat, almost as an admission of the *production* they're embarking on, the movie-like nature of their endeavour. It might be a similar stretch, but it's obvious to consider the final scene in the Hackman film, in which the wounded boat spirals and cannot escape its own irrevocable vortex…?

It is intriguing that Rosenbaum finds even the potential ambiguities within *Night Moves* (which he admits abound in the film) to be boring. Glossing over his challenge to not be boring with any of our thoughts about *Night Moves*, the very citation of boredom seems relevant to the discussion of genre expectations (and indeed the implications of Justin Chang's comment about duration and the go-to descriptor of 'slowness'). This may be in part because the way the characters are drawn, they do themselves seem bored with much of what is happening (even their own scheme at times), so I'm intrigued. My attention is also piqued by the tone of the film at different points. Having read the articles you linked to (thank you!) and having a better sense of the intriguing consistencies and connections with Reichardt's previous films (still to be caught up on), I was thinking about how the build-up/unravelling form of *Night Moves* carries within it a non-localised hinge between a first half—similarly rooted in a "present tense making things unforeseeable", as Rosenbaum describes *Meek's Cutoff*—and a second half that swings into a nauseatingly helpless and desperate retrospection, as things cannot be undone. This isn't quite a tonal shift like in *From Dusk Til Dawn*, ahem, but I'd find it worthwhile to consider how the filmmakers realise such differences of urgency and direction as the film unfolds—shifting through an active present pre-explosion, a bubble of satisfaction (Josh risking a smile when looking out the ceiling porthole of his cell-like yurt) immediately morphing into a paralysed phase of paranoia, fear (and regret?), only to falsely resolve into another active present in the attempt to regain control in fatal violence.

Thinking of this 'presentness' of the first half (and its relation to genre convention), I recall that the trio's plan is not articulated in advance, either for each other or for the benefit of audience. They don't lay it out with diagrams and a team talk à la Danny Ocean and co. Instead we (the audience) are dropped in to attend to them from the wings as they make their preparations, without exposition, if not in silence. We become the characters' silent accomplices, fellow travellers. Watching preparations that range from the danger-tinged to the bucolic, from the nocturnally wild to the mundane and prosaic. We are a far cry from supervillains grandstanding or laying out the intricate beauty of their scheme-in-motion. Yet it seems to me that one thing that Reichardt gleefully borrows from the genre-jelly in these sections is a portrait (albeit peculiarly rendered, both tender and hollow) of the camaraderie of the heist: the setting of problems and their solutions, divisions of labour, production lines, even if the writer/director lays innumerable booby traps, false notes, comedic lapses—from not having enough fertilizer or getting café opening times wrong, to not being able to reset the charge—that could have been warnings or escape routes. Again, the focused thrill of the targeted activity is shot through with the tacit genre expectations that have trickled down through cinema, television, etc. and which flow through the characters as much as they do the audience who watch them. (Consider *Four Lions* or the more recent *The Order.*) But as you have suggested, what gets set up here (partially undercut by the strained interpersonal disjunctions that impart the hollow tone) is a sense of how the provisional efficacy of such collective action nonetheless rings false in the open air of reality. There is a near-innocent attitude at work in these early scenes, still at the point where an 'internal' plan remains intact before it is enacted in the world, which I particularly enjoy. I love scenes like this in literature too: the making of lists, setting quantities, recon, shopping excursions, backstories, choreography; scenes where our heroes go to stores with intent, engaging with the possibility that everything they need to solve their problems can be affordably bought here and now—to build the bomb, to get rid of the body, tools for both perpetrating and cleaning up criminal acts and violent ends. These are often rendered in shots of superstore aisles, stock-rich and specialist, often peculiarly American in scale, a heady mixture of access and excess. One wonders how this familiar trope (and underlying reality) of commercial privilege gives birth to a *certain kind of planning*... perhaps even exposing it to greater risk of apathy and oversight? I might be going way off-piste here, but there you go. One cannot help but recall that the ending puts us right back in the store—but as you say, that's getting way ahead of ourselves.

Given your incisive distinction between conse-quence and aftermath, I wondered about a scene I noticed more on my recent second viewing, which contained the ostensibly cliché-ridden exchange between Dena and Josh respectively: "You said no one would get hurt." [*loaded pause*] "What did you think was going to happen?" Although this acknowledges that they did indeed give cursory thought to potential consequences, more interestingly the dynamic of the later exchange suggests that they continued to under-estimate them and retrospectively accept them at the same time. It is also a telling moment in the very specific pairing of Josh and Dena as near-theatrical archetypes: one overly sullen and serious (to the point of discomfort), the other seemingly chipper in the face of the end of the world (until her body betrays her). Much more on all this later no doubt (as well as the huge subject of how gender is explored in the film) but one wonders if they're not a two-part, hybrid Raskolnikov…

Working with shared purpose by no means implies a shared resilience. Or that your suffering will be shared or even held in common. Reactions are not shop-bought, just as you cannot get inside someone else's skull. For ton of bricks read iceberg, as the extent of one's plan always lies beneath the surface. Once one's responsibility irrevocably extends beyond any stated intention, we see how a person's full attitude to their initial plan—after its witnessed impact in the world, once you don't recognise it—takes shape in another plan (one you are forced to conceive and enact without allies).

Anyway. So, the opening scene. The use of sound—which we have yet to mention—is flagged here, as the low industrial rumble of the dam pipe comes before anything—distant cause, impossible foe. The first shot is the pressure valve at the base of the dam, briefly still before flaring into high-pressure spray, which then amplifies with great force. This is major infrastructure, a military-grade target. Our two main characters are then photographed on their own—a play of distance and proximity that runs throughout the film, where one overrides the other, denoting ease or estrangement, unrequited yearning or indifference, etc. Josh looks down, vertiginously, to the outlet pipe. He is hunched and pensive, uptight. Similarly ready to blow. The first shot of Dena shows a physicality that is very different: she is cornered but open, like a boxer resting between rounds. She turns away. She is interested in looking around, Josh not so much. The scoping exercise makes one wonder about the lack of security or surveillance on the dam—no doubt why it was being chosen. But when does this scene take place in the chronology? Is this the original reconnaissance mission? Before or after its selection? Why would they need to revisit? Is one of them being caught up, drafted into the scheme?

A few lines of dialogue, low in the mix, quickly damn the dam (sorry), citing its lack of fish ladders as both an indictment of inadequate regulation and an implicit suggestion of corruption ("Wonder how they got around that?"—something that foreshadows the character burning his cheese license later in the film: setting up a conflict between good rule breaking and bad; was it Mike Gatting in 1987: "One rule for one, one for another"… again, sorry). It also sets out a tetchy dynamic between Josh and Dena when he corrects her with an upgrade of "vacuums".* Even the seemingly simple shot of the pair walking alongside the fence, heads out of shot, seems telling. Josh leads Dena and she cannot help but touch and test each section of the metal mesh, as if restless, keen to play or make light. Am I imagining it, or does the sound make Josh half-turn, as if contemplating telling her to shut up (which he will do many times throughout the film, a thread of sexism and condescension we'll no doubt get to)? One thinks of "Please don't move so much, Alma" expanding into "It's entirely too much movement at breakfast" in *Phantom Thread*. Having exited through a conspicuous hole in the fence, Dena is then shocked to hear an oriole, and her excited "I didn't know we had those" might suggest a naïve ignorance, but more tellingly the "we" claims an identification that is uncertain (and arguably will remain so). Her origins are suggested to be in Connecticut, with expensive schooling in New York, but the offhand "we" speaks more of an implied commonality, a common good, for which many things can be put at risk.

Am keen to hear your thoughts and assume you will tackle the sauna scenes?

---

* See https://www.oregonlive.com/environment/2023/11/this-billion-dollar-plan-to-save-salmon-depends-on-a-giant-fish-vacuum.html.

Letter four

Dear David,

I'll see if I can keep this one a bit shorter so we can get a bit of a back-and-forth rhythm going, though brevity isn't always my strong point. You've made it easy for me because I pretty much agree wholeheartedly with everything you say in your last letter.

Three things I just want to repeat so as to bookmark them: the "hinge" is a great way of describing the crucial turn in the film's form. Nicole Brenez has written about this kind of thing in relation to Abel Ferrara. She claims that his films use one of two strategies, being either "organized upon a single major fold, where the beginning finally meets or 'touches' the ending", or alternatively "a more gradual pleat, where the major fold is progressively translated throughout in a series of small folds… over the entire structure of a film".[*] *Night Moves* seems to be an instance of the former device, but possibly the idea of a collection of smaller folds will also prove useful here. I also want to say—to get ahead of ourselves again, which is proving so hard to avoid—that absolutely crucial to the central hinge is the unexpected surge of self-pity (unexpected as much by Josh as by the audience), which changes the texture of everything. Secondly I want to say how great the phrase "a two-part, hybrid Raskolnikov" is. And finally you're so right to emphasise the importance of shops. It puts me in mind of *Double Indemnity*, although possibly by contrast as much as similarity. Those scenes of Barbara Stanwyck and Fred MacMurray hiding their meetings in plain sight use the shop as a pretext; what's so devastating for Josh at the end of the film is that that's precisely what he's unable

---

[*] Nicole Brenez (trans. Adrian Martin), *Abel Ferrara* (University of Illinois Press, 2007), p. 15.

to do. (He *needs* a job and to disappear, but neither are possible—and certainly not simultaneously.)

On the opening scene: I like the idea that "one of them is being caught up, drafted into the scheme" very much. Surely it's Dena being drafted, isn't it? I'm quite prepared to accept that "the sound make[s] Josh half-turn, as if contemplating telling her to shut up". And about birds on different coasts, I wonder if this is a piece of gentle self-mockery on Reichardt's part. She's talked about how she used bird sounds from a recording in *Old Joy* only to be told by ornithologists that they were all east coast birds that one could never encounter in Oregon! But since I feel I have to disagree with *something*, I'll put a question mark on the idea that "[w]e become the characters' silent accomplices, fellow travellers." The fact that they initiated their plans without us being around to see and hear them doing it renders this not exactly the right description, I think. To begin with we don't know what they're doing, which is surely a necessary condition for being an accomplice.

I find the ensuing sauna scene a little perplexing. (What's in the brown paper bag that Dena gives Josh?) I suppose one thing that this scene does, upon subsequent viewings, is to rhyme with the later, frightening scenes that take place there between Josh and Dena as things start to fall apart. (Perhaps an example of the film's smaller-scale folds or hinges?) The editing throughout the whole film up to this point has a very subtly destabilising mix of clarity and obscurity. For example, it quickly becomes clear where Josh is standing on the dam in relation to the pipe. But where exactly is Dena in relation to him when we first see her? In the sauna Josh seems clearly to be looking at the bathing women, but the lack of a shot showing them together complicates this. He could also, just possibly, not really be seeing them, caught up in his own thoughts.

He's clearly irritated, though: there's the way he elbows the door closed, plus his obvious contempt for the hippie-Buddhist trappings of the place, as expressed in the Hitler moustache he draws on the man surrounded by Om symbols on the cover of the "life coaching" brochure. He apparently finds it uncomfortable to stay outside in proximity to the naked middle-aged women ("You didn't wait", Dena tells him), but why exactly? (Are there psychoanalytic threads to be followed here?) Is he irritated directly *by* what he finds in the sauna, or is it rather that it's exacerbating his nervous tension, rather than being the immediate source of his mood? I'm not sure. Either way, there's a sense of emotional disproportion here which I think is important.

I'm also not sure if I'm right to be reminded of Robert Altman's *3 Women*. Is there more to say than that these are two films that foreground therapeutic bathing early on? Certainly that's another film with a very prominent hinge or fold. Is there any suggestion that there's much more in common between Josh and Dena and Shelley Duvall's blithely unworldly Millie (who—at least at the start of the film—takes herself for the very epitome of worldly experience) than we might assume?

Letter five

Dear Dom,
     Much to mull here. I think you're right to question my suggestion of the audience becoming 'accomplices' and wondered if a better term would be 'accessories' but even that's not quite right, despite there being something interesting about potential differences between 'before…' and 'after the fact'. Strangely, I had half a mind on Beckett's 'Auditor' from *Not I*, but not sure that's any clearer. Despite the stage directions for that hooded figure's four movements—"simple sideways raising of arms from sides and their falling back, in a gesture of helpless compassion [that] lessens with each recurrence till scarcely perceptible at third"—being quite relevant to my experience of watching *Night Moves*, I'm not sure it's worth dwelling on.
     I found the Brenez quotes on fold and pleat structures in Ferrara's films fascinating and feel that both are absolutely relevant to what Reichardt is doing. I briefly glanced at an online copy of the book and was struck by another phrase from the same section: "passing from the recto to the verso of a given situation or image", which also seemed applicable to representations of given characters and their capacities, how they might be seen to turn inside-out, or undergo some kind of transformation, whether it be Dena's physical (unavoidably readable) manifestation or Josh's internalised one (which he tries to keep illegible). Something here reminds me of Catherine Malabou's writing on plasticity—which she approaches, to put it very broadly, as the giving and receiving of form—particularly when she contrasts a notion of metamorphosis as change in form whilst an underlying substance is maintained, with what she calls destructive plasticity, in which transformation is irreversible—a kind of trau-

matic rupture with the past and a reconfiguration of an entirely new being. I picked up her *Ontology of the Accident* and there was a quote that made me think of both Dena and Josh, and even a sense of multiple pleats building up: "The change may equally well emerge from apparently anodyne events which ultimately prove to be veritable traumas inflecting the course of a life, producing the metamorphosis of someone about whom one says: 'I would never have guessed that they would end up like that'."[*] Although the events we witness are not anodyne (!), when we leave Josh at the end of the film, we may well wonder *where* the changes occurred. Or (remembering *something* from my inexplicable statistics A-level) whether the train of events formed a discrete or continuous *distribution…*? Perhaps the ending is so particular because his transformation is elastic (rather than destructively plastic) and he returns to himself. He doesn't fully become a monster but carries one in him. A plan can go that far wrong.

On the facing page, I noticed Brenez drawing a contrast between the 'fatalistic' and the 'tragic' in relation to attitudes to pervasive *evil* in Ferrara's films (!!). This also seemed to have relevance to the thematic substructure of *Night Moves*: climate breakdown, immense and ungraspable disaster, and the imperative (and inability) to respond to it. Brenez suggests that the fatalistic attitude demands a "frontal description of the disaster" (which might tie in with David Denby's claim that Reichardt's tone in *Night Moves* is "glumly objective") and that the tragic maintains a position of resistance whilst knowing that it is "doomed to failure".[†]

---

[*] Catherine Malabou (trans. Carolyn Shread), *Ontology of the Accident: An Essay on Destructive Plasticity* (Polity Press, 2012) p. 6.
[†] 'Disconnected Man', *The New Yorker*, 2 June 2014 and Brenez, *op. cit.*, p. 14.

Despite being something of a rehash of the theatrical archetypes idea, this is potentially useful in thinking about Josh, Dena, and the film as a whole. Again, I suspect a mixture of both attitudes is in play—a recipe for black humour perhaps—and that its tragic-fatalistic action takes place in the face of Sisyphean futility; or, as Brenez puts it (in an entirely different context, admittedly) that within a depicted cinematic reality, 'good' actions—from the ostensibly noble to the morally compromised—"have no efficacy".[*]

I agree about the strangeness of the bathhouse scene. The whole scenario actually reminded me of certain Japanese prints, often noted for complex and illogical perspectives.[†] The shots of bathers that Josh 'sees' do appear to be entirely distinct vignettes impossible for him to scan from a singular position. I'm keen to watch *3 Women*—one might also think of the strangeness of the bathhouse in *Spirited Away* or, dare I say it, a Lynchian lodge—and there is surely something deliberate in the location's rarefied atmosphere, a self-contained series of worlds that not only speaks (for Josh?) of luxury, apathy and inaction, but also as altered spaces in which the atmosphere is heightened and exaggerated—your 'emotional disproportion' is great—whether it be a site of disorientation where identities slip and dissolve, or a microcosm of the suffocating hothouse Earth that is the underlying endgame of the disaster. Surely more to say, too, about the motif of water throughout the film—in different aggregate states, held at bay, allowed to flood, etc.

The brown paper bag presumably contains the money for the boat?

---

[*] Brenez, *op. cit.*, p. 14.
[†] See https://www.artic.edu/artworks/36550/women-s-bathhouse-and-laundry.

We cut to an outdoor scene, following close behind a young boy freewheeling down a mud track into a lush autumnal Oregon valley. We glimpse the isolated cooperative farm in front of forested hills. The camera is loose, as if similarly bike-bound, in an easeful descent into beauty and isolation. A vibe of containment, self-sufficiency. A little knit of colours in the bright yellow jacket and blue bike frame, the journey only stopped when the faded yellow of an idle JCB is reached. We cut to the first instance of a type of framing I noticed with great pleasure on my initial watch: a heavily tilted image of two young workers (Dylan and Surprise) harvesting vegetables, one standing, the other on their knees. If it weren't for the slope, one might be put in mind of a Millet, or some other 'brown painting' depiction of people labouring in fields. The slope declares precarity one suspects. The field boundary, where it meets forest scrub behind it, pretty much bisects the screen from bottom left to top right. There is a sense of raw land being made productive without being commandeered—these are not heavily engineered Inca terraces, but rather scenes of low-impact farming, adaptive, sympathetic. A reverse shot: a straw-filled, roof racked pickup tipped alarmingly on the opposite angle. There is no visible horizon line to know how much the slant is exaggerated by the shot or simply a mark of the terrain. From the van (but out of shot), Sean (Kai Lennox) asks about the absent Josh, who has taken a walk, already disengaging.

We then cut to solitary Josh, or rather his hands, as we watch him pick up a bird's nest from the forest floor and gently place it into the low branches of a tree. I confess, I find this a bit much. It seems hokey, laughable, if not tongue-through-cheek. I wonder if Reichardt held her nose when keeping it in. On some level I know it's necessary, but still. This and the deer add up to something perhaps? But the scene gets subtly stranger. We move ahead of Josh, watching him walk pensively through the brush. We are not shown what he is looking at (his gaze already de-stablised by the bathhouse stares) but he is puzzled, intent. Actually, it's an odd mix of expressions… Eisenberg's saccadic acting. I strained for the sound, underneath the weave of soundtrack tones, footfall and birdsong, of a low hum that could conceivably be a river or a distant roadway. I feel there is a sense of Josh discovering something for the first time, as if we watch him discern the limits of his sanctuary: the co-operative farm, a last refuge of community for the spiralling misanthrope perhaps, is being encroached upon, and is under threat like everything else. Another pleat here, another nail in the coffin. The voiceover from the next scene playing over the shot seems to confirm this, yet the emphasis on vision is striking, perhaps more so than the urgency: "The disaster we see is happening everywhere at the same time. The clock is ticking".

Letter six

Dear David,
     Funnily enough, I have no problem at all with Josh picking up the bird's nest, I think because I assume what we're supposed to take from it has to do with how Josh sees himself—that there is a preposterousness in the self-importance that he confuses for selflessness—rather than with how the film sees him. I grant, though, that the distinction is treacherous, if perhaps less dangerous than it would be to mark the separation between film and character too clearly so early in the film. The earlier shot following the boy on his bike is the first one that I find ever so slightly disappointing. Something, perhaps, to do with the way the landscape shifts with the moving camera and combines with the gentle piano soundtrack to too-clearly signal that this is a healthier environment than the hot springs? I can't really justify my feeling, which is the tiniest of quibbles anyway, but it has persisted on repeated viewings.
     I haven't yet found Malabou as rewarding as so many others seem to. (The Aristotelian in me resists the distinction between "a notion of metamorphosis as change in form whilst an underlying substance is maintained, with what she calls destructive plasticity, in which transformation is irreversible"; surely a change in form isn't a *change* unless there is some continuity of substance; whether it is reversible or not is, I think, a separate question.) But the question of where to pinpoint the changes in the film—particularly in Josh— is an excellent one to raise. If we manage to locate them, that doesn't of course mean that their results were inevitable (that would be to confuse the intelligibility of the past with determinism, something Malabou's great influence G.W.F. Hegel has often been accused of). It does certainly seem that the film goes out of its way to

make those moments hard to identify and isolate. But I think interpreting this correctly is a delicate matter; I don't think we should see it as a sign of relativism or scepticism. Nor, however, should we conclude with Denby that *Night Moves* is "glumly objective", which sounds to me as if it presents us only with surfaces. I think Reichardt's filmmaking agrees with Wittgenstein that we can *see* anger (say) in a face, rather than just evidence for the existence of anger. But things get really difficult—and really interesting—when such a position engages with situations when it is genuinely difficult to see what's going on.

A darkened room that has been turned into a makeshift theatre in which a group of mostly young activists are watching the end of a competent, if unremarkable, piece of environmental activist filmmaking—"let the revolution begin!"—complete with pedestrian soft rock soundtrack, credited to one Jackie Christianson (it was actually made by Larry Fessenden, a colleague of Reichardt's since *River of Grass* days). We see cutaways of people watching intently, some of whom we know (Dena), some of whom we do not. One of them, Katherine Waterston's Anne, will later become a character, albeit a minor one. She whispers something to Dena, who gives a slightly half-hearted smile. I'm not quite sure why; a reminder of the different ways in which messages can be shared, as well as of the limits concerning who they can be shared with, perhaps? A private joke is not merely a joke that only a few people happen to have heard.

As the film ends, Josh sighs to himself indulgently. He clearly thinks (well, clearly on repeated viewings, I think) that the film is a poor substitute for the braver action he has in mind: he's going to practice what the film merely preaches. A short debate ensues about whether being too direct about the scale of the crisis could be counterproductive, conveying the message that, as one man puts it, "it's too late". If Brenez is right that the tragic maintains a position of resistance whilst knowing that it is "doomed to failure" then it is hard to see how action in the face of the climate emergency could be anything other than tragic. But this doesn't seem quite right—and not necessarily for encouraging reasons, because there are worse things than tragedy (self-deluding fatalistic complacency, for example). When Dena asks Jackie what she thinks they should do, her answer is that "one big plan" thinking is part of the problem. Which is precisely what Josh also thinks; we see him, I think, at least partially reconsidering his earlier exasperation.

This might seem a fairly functional and unremarkable scene, but I think it's a difficult one; there are many ways it could have gone wrong, tipping the film's hand—commenting on its own narrative—too crudely or too obviously. It's interesting that Reichardt doesn't opt for a documentary style here; we don't, except in a couple of wider shots, feel like members of the audience—there's little sense of placing us in the space when we are shown the single shots of individual figures. Perhaps it's scenes like this that suggested glum objectivity to Denby. But what strikes me is how different this scene is than the rest of the film; if *Night Moves* addressed the question of whether bombing a dam is a justifiable response to the climate crisis, more of it might have been like this. Perhaps that's the point.

Letter seven

Dear Dom,

On the surface, the subsequent scene might seem similarly unremarkable, even minor in the scheme of things, yet it might be worth lingering over. For one thing, considering how the transition to the previous screening scene had been staggered, there is an abruptness to the edit here. The audio cuts off—"sharing our concerns in one"—almost as if the unfinished statement hinting at unified collective action (however it is to be pursued) is specifically dismissed, jettisoned from this point on. Whether this relates to any given route the film will take, or if it's an insight into characters' attitudes, assumed positions, resolution, etc., we might leave open for now. Yet given the secretive nature of their imminent guerrilla action, the edit seems to emphasise the idea that the break they're committed to making is conscious, contemptuous even, and that they are already closed off to any bland statements of action (more endless talk) they associate with such activist groups. In their minds decisions have been made. Appointments need to be kept. They are now the radical faction, given power through secrecy. And with such secrets comes the boldness of clique and a tacit wherewithal that provides a whole hidden choreographic substructure for such things as sighs, smirks, glances, and silences.

All that said, the violence of the cut is typically (and instantly) undercut by absurdity. We cut to the view from the cab of Josh's truck, sat in traffic at some non-descript intersection—the sound of nearby construction, an array of commercial banners festooning the verges (SUPERCUTS!)—startlingly framed around a mascot cow dancing on the sidewalk. Hawking 'Wilbur Milk, made by Happy Local Cows', the figure jigs and waves at the stationary motorists, as we listen to Josh and Dena start to discuss their errand. Made more jarring by the switch from the darkness of the makeshift cinema to the synthetic overload of dayglo commercial signage, the image is one of the more obviously anomalous moments in the film. (It does have a strange echo with the talkative character who runs into our trio in the lakeside woods and struggles to make conversation in a near-Wes-Anderson farce—another flag for the subject of humour in the film.) The dancing cow would seem to be an emblematic plant the director is embracing gleefully (there's even an arrow pointing at it: metaphor here!) to shorthand all manner of things: the humiliation of nature; clowning commercial language; the cynicism, complicity and inescapability amid coagulating junkspace; localism as a riposte to the destructive impact of the US dairy industry's megafarms, etc.

But it is a brief vision. We snap out of the fever dream of consumer Armageddon as the camera switches to view Dena and Josh side by side in the truck (seemingly watching the dancing cow—which never progresses past the cab and potentially never leaves their sight). We come to understand that they are on their way to buy the boat. The scene's simple framing of frontal views of passenger and driver helps to contrast their respective demeanours and attitudes at this stage of their plan. Dena assumes the unnerving, fatalistic calm of a person who has embraced the "end-of-world vision" decried during the DIY film screening. In fact, the prefacing of her question seemed a direct expression of this: "Yah, end of the world, what's there really to lose…"—the tumbled, rhetorical phrasing of which betraying an implied (self-given) permission to separate means from ends. Behind the wheel, Josh is more obviously stiffened by neurotic anxiety, ostensibly about logistics, not wanting to be late to meet Dena's contact. When she suggests calling to mitigate against this, his slightly odd reply—"I don't want to find a payphone right now"—for me becomes another strange point of humour. For one thing, it again emphasises how Reichardt centres the film on the human investments within the 'procedural', showing how the smallest logistical inconveniences (brought about by secrecy, covering one's tracks, or stepping out of the 'system' in any small way) can become a source of humiliation and frustration, as part of an attempt to interweave the shape and intent of a disruptive plan into everyday life. (I suppose it's an obvious point, already made, to state that the film is 'procedural' in genre. Denby even suggests that what obsesses Reichardt is "not why they launch the attack but how" [perhaps linked to the fact that her father was a crime scene detective]. Still, his claim that the film's failure to give any account of *how* "virtuous types" [in his rather sniffy phrase] turn to violent destruction is a "hole in the movie" actually seems like a particularly compelling notion around which to structure a film from the outset.) Yet the way Josh's line prompts a particular response from Dena seems subtle and rich. His strangely Woody Allen-like answer—which to me sounds like the punchline to a joke that hasn't been set up quite right—produces the tiniest of smiles across her lips, barely pinching enough to change shape, before a just-audible snort comes, located more in the upper chest than an expressive face. Josh's paranoia, his inability to manoeuvre between worry about problems and their solutions, are laughable at this point. And Dena needs to be the anarchic adult and remind him how to function: "Breathe, Josh". There is another kind of contempt latent here, one might suggest, a tiny revenge for the belittling we see more and more of. In this passing moment, barely perceptible amid the flotsam and jetsam of consciousness, she thinks he's ridiculous. Her "All's well", especially accompanied by the raised tilt of the capped head, seemed strangely dissociated and *constructed*. But at this point, she's enjoying it. He isn't.

Letter eight

Dear David,

And then we're outside a large suburban house with both a truck and a big people-carrier visible in the garage. Dena is up a stepladder looking at a boat, rather handsomely painted in off-white and a claretty red. The middle-aged male owner is describing its virtues with the texture of *Star Trek* technobabble ("inboard, five-litre V8 engine" isn't, for me, too far from talk of dilithium crystals; and I think perhaps not for Josh and Dena either, given that Harmon later seems much more knowledgeable in this area). The owner reminisces over the fact that the boat gave him a "lot of good skiing". (Water-skiing, obviously.) As he repeats this Josh emerges from the inside of the boat and, towering above both of them, unceremoniously interrupts and asks if he can use the bathroom.

I'm not entirely sure why, or whether, Josh does so. (It's ambiguous as to whether he actually has a pee or not.) Surely going inside generates entirely unnecessary risk. (Other people might see Josh and be able to recognise him later.) Josh looks around the home, all done up in utterly bland good taste. The camera's pan from right to left emphasises the theme of water resources, from the artificial waterfall visible out of the window, to the television above the fireplace showing a golfer about to take a swing. (Thus the idea of golf, which will later lead to an important little irony, is introduced.) I get the impression that Josh mainly wants to go into the house so that he can indulge in some contempt for its owner. (You're quite right about Dena enjoying things, and Josh not, in the previous scene, but here he is enjoying not enjoying it.) He briefly spies on Dena and the owner from the first-floor window, sustaining the paranoid mood. As Josh and Dena drive off, he pointedly refuses to join in her role-play ("Can't believe this is happening, right honey?"), as if it's beneath him. But Josh's failure to respond and rather tetchy-sounding slamming of the door of the truck gives a perfectly convincing impression of a couple whose argument has been inconveniently interrupted by having to go off and buy a boat.

They drive off through stunningly wooded hills, and then suddenly it's night. There is a conversation about what "close" is. There follows the scene with the deer, which we've already discussed. It's now clear that this relates both to the person dressed up as the dancing cow (are all animals in films somehow "dressed up"?), and to the film's self-awareness of its use of metaphor. (Great spot of the arrow in the dancing cow scene, by the way!) And then they have arrived. Harmon (Peter Sarsgaard) appears, bearded and smiling, in the headlights. He raises his arms in some kind of hieratic greeting, then walks backwards to let them drive further forward. It's suddenly like a horror film: the old friend who the protagonists haven't seen for ages invites them to his cabin in the woods and turns out to have gone insane in the interim. We discover that Harmon and Dena are meeting for the first time ("You must be D"; "You're the infamous H"). He shines the torch in her face, less so as to see her better as to temporarily blind her, to goof around and gain an epistemic advantage. Both of them are introduced to one another in a beam of electric light. I'm not quite sure how to read that.

Harmon remarks ironically on the boat's name: "*Night Moves*! Slick!" Dena declares it to have been better than the other choices: *Gone Fishin'*; *Wet Dream*; *Makin' Waves*; *Reel Wild*; *Jamaican Me Crazy*; *Gone With the Wind*. For a moment we might almost think that she and Josh did choose the name (we haven't yet had a clear view of the back of the boat where the name is now emblazoned), but this seems pretty unlikely; what Dena's doing is, once again, displaying her skill at improvisation. Josh cuts off what he sees as her tiresome indulgence with familiar impatience ("all right"), ironically not recognizing how vital this ability will be later on (the important fertilizer-buying scene). (Although later on things change: one could describe the last third of the film as about failure to improvise, as well as about failures *of* improvisation.) But though there may be ironic non-recognition here, there is also plenty of recognition of irony: Harmon is able to joke about the fact that if they weren't going to blow up the boat it would have "years left in her" — "I guess we don't give a shit about longevity, do we" — as well as about their paranoia: "There's narcs everywhere around here", he tells Josh, "and don't trust the raccoons at all". Dena's ability to share this view of the funny side connects her to Harmon and distinguishes her from Josh. Just before he makes the remark about the raccoons, Josh and Harmon walk away from the boat, Harmon's arm around Josh, and the shot is held for a surprisingly long time. Greenish and red lights constitute an almost abstract composition rather than illuminating anything much. Stop or go?

Letter nine

Dear Dom,

The subsequent scene inside Harmon's mobile home, somewhere 'far out' if not completely off grid, features the most dialogue so far—and sees the three co-conspirators converse more fully. The interior is dark, intimate, although evenly lit compared with the deep contrasts and light shows outside. Josh and Dena's nocturnal arrival actually reminded me of the ad hoc discovery of rough ground—an upturned sofa picked out by a cone of headlights—that provides the makeshift campsite in *Old Joy*—the intended destination having remained doubtful in its close ties with a key character's flakiness.

Still, the trio is together now, so there is a sense that things might shift up a gear. Handed new ID cards from a tin—the preparation of which clearly having been one of Harmon's tasks—our two leads contemplate new identities. From tomorrow, Dena will be 'Carrie Taylor', a name that touches on some unexplained connection for Harmon and Josh—a person they both know perhaps, or even, given the reaction, a former flame? If there's a wider cultural reference or joke here, it's passing me by. Yet there's a subtle skill in how Reichardt does this kind of thing, I think, offering up a passing intimacy through quite believable fragments of speech, yet not allowing them to settle or deepen. She's willing to hint at other stories we won't get, to sketch out openings and closures yet skip over them like the lacunae that pepper everyday conversation. Perhaps it is similar to the kind of private joke we saw Dena share in the cinema scene, but here expressed in another kind of register, one that is more juvenile, insecure, and revealing?

Dena's wit emerges again in this scene, at first seeking to subtly undermine Josh's programmatic roll-call of "Joseph Marker, 10-30-81" (does the surname sound like 'mocker'? Is he the 'mark'?), immediately shortening him to the "Joey" he has always been. She then extends Harmon's "Ed" moniker—which for some reason I cannot help but associate with Mister Ed, as if he later becomes a prompting horse, devil on the shoulder, even if disembodied on the phone— through reference to talk show hosts McMahon and Sullivan (promoting Harmon from sidekick to main man as she goes) before wittily reframing 'Joey' as 'Joe McCarthy'... a stronger tease of his paranoia and a jab decent enough that she laughs at it by herself. Her sense of humour has been starved of a sparring partner, hence the connection to Harmon.

The subject of golf, which you flagged in the unattended TV images in the boat buying scene, comes back in relation to mention of the number of courses popping up in the area of Bend, Oregon (a specific location that might tip us off in terms of 'how close is close'), mentioned by Harmon as a poisonous symptom of what they're up against. Backed up with a pleasingly surreal throwaway description—"taxidermy, gourmet food, $8 coffee"—the theme of water is emphasised in the incredulous disgust at the artificial irrigation necessary to sustain golf links in the Oregon High Desert—which, if not an actual desert, is an arid, elevated territory of shrubland and steppe. Oddly enough, this connection brought home to me the stark shift of setting from the Arizona / Utah canyons of Edward Abbey's *The Monkey Wrench Gang* (1975)— which, of course, was the subject of a (later settled) copyright lawsuit in relation to *Night Moves*, which we have yet to mention—to the relative lushness of green Oregon. Having now read Abbey's novel, there's much to say about it, similarities and differences, but perhaps not here...

When our trio return to discussing their plan, they come to the first setback so far, as Harmon reveals a 500lb shortfall in the fertilizer he had been tasked with acquiring. The way the script brings in his subsistence job excuse—"those greens don't mow themselves"—is a deliciously funny line that taps into so much irony and compromised self-awareness, hubris and hypocrisy, collusion and complicity, necessary evils, and so forth. Actually, there's an interesting echo here with Abbey's character, George Hayduke—a former Marine no less—and his plan of getting "into the heart of that motherfucker...", referring to the Glen Canyon Dam on the Colorado River, which the quartet of activists intend (but fail) to destroy over the course of the novel. At the very end of the book, the presumed-dead Hayduke reappears and claims to have a job as a security guard at the dam, opening up future opportunities for its destruction. He had contemplated this strategy earlier in the book too, figuring that he might clean up his appearance and get a job within a construction company, in order to then "bore from within, like the noble cutworm".* Sensibly or not, the idea occurs to me that Reichardt may have been thinking of *Night Moves* as a peculiar sequel to Abbey's book, one that presses harder for results, and indeed consequences, which Abbey only flirts with. But Harmon's working on the golf course seems a different kind of insertion, in any case. His further evasion is also pretty funny, as he tries to convince the others that the pressures upon the (female!) dam mean that it wants to collapse—therefore requiring less explosive force—stirring a strangely moral, weirdly gendered, anthropomorphism into the

---

* Edward Abbey, *The Monkey Wrench Gang* (London: Penguin Classics, 1975), p. 104.

mix. And something that makes you wonder about what happens to Dena over the course of the film.

But the need for more fertilizer is a problem, and Josh's concern that buying any more than 10lbs sets off red flags makes it quite stark. Given what we've said so far, I find myself looking for cracks in Josh. Another interesting flip is buried here: as if taken unawares by his immediate agreement with Dena's pointed criticism of Harmon—"We should have known about this earlier"—Josh instantaneously reverts to condescension, almost desperately asserting himself by shutting her up: she might be right but he needs to be right-er. Dena absorbs this puerility by distracting herself with the freshly laminated identity on the table. Josh's subsequent hand gesture—finger to the temple, a little like Brad Pitt giving it full tortured ham on the psych ward in *12 Monkeys*—as he reluctantly agrees to try buying more fertilizer in the morning, suggests a range of underlying stress points and physical symptoms. He clearly does not respond well to setbacks.

Come to think of it, it was striking during the boat buying scene how Josh seemed to slip from super cautious paranoia in the truck to a kind of blasé judgmental rudeness, barely feigning to entertain the fiction Dena improvises with the seller and, as you say, becoming needlessly memorable in the process. There are subtle moments when the flimsy fiction could have crumbled: Josh being pulled back outside after he hears (or does he?) Dena being asked which supermarket he works at. The energy could easily have turned here—red flag central—as why on earth would the guy give a shit? It is left to Dena to back up the improvisation (to stop the rot, to normalise his behaviour), which we don't see. There's also the clear flash of unease on the boat owner's face when holding the wedge of cash in his hands, as if weighing up whether he's been hoodwinked, involved a drug deal, or party to something else he could barely predict.

Still, the plan is reset, finds a new plateau. They will buy more, everything is fine.

One last thing. I find the layered ironies, double standards, and complexities in Harmon's "longevity" comment also deliciously rich, especially as it reflects and shimmers amid the overall duration of the film. I find myself questioning just how self-aware they are, or the degree to which they are compromised despite their cause being urgent. And the images of their fatal commitment to and investment in broader sustainability, memorably undercut for me in the landfill scene to come.

Letter ten

Dear David,

The conversation between Harmon, Josh, and Dena in the trailer, together with the subsequent few scenes, are a rigorous formal study of conversation in film. The three-way conversation in the trailer that you've discussed consists entirely of one-shots, each of them showing one of the characters framed centrally and unfussily. We know that the characters are sitting in a triangle—Harmon is to Dena's left, Josh to her right—but we know this purely from the characters' eyelines, the directions in which they look while talking to one another. So far, so classical—this is the kind of thing that could easily go unnoticed. And yet if one *does* notice it, it starts to become—entirely appropriately to the film's theme and tone—just a little oppressive, somewhat claustrophobic. A wider shot of the interior, or a two-shot, would be perfectly possible, even given the constrained surroundings of the trailer, but the film refuses any such oxygenating variation.

Is this "classical" or not? I don't find it easy to decide, nor to decide to what extent this is a helpful question or not. Certainly the idea—surprisingly commonly voiced—that Reichardt is some kind of anti-classicist, working doggedly with extended duration and some kind of sheer (non)-event rather than with narrative, character, continuity editing, and the like, is simply false. But then again, not many Hollywood films from the '40s (say) would stick so relentlessly to the three one-shots as Reichardt does here. So one could say that the film's form at this point is in dialogue with a kind of classicism, invoking it but also, by means of its very relentlessness, also drawing attention to the differences of this film's language. And yet, as I've noted, it only draws attention to itself

if you notice it—if saying that isn't simply contradic-
tory! And such stylistic self-effacement is supposed
to be precisely what marks out classical filmmaking
as such.

The stylistic interrogation continues. First we get
a very classical shot/reverse-shot of Josh and Dena
having a face-to-face conversation about her mistrust
of Harmon, outside. This is followed by a conversation,
back in the trailer again, between Josh and Harmon.
Again we have a strict alternation of one-shots with
nothing to vary the pattern, but this time the two men
are facing in opposite directions, their gazes parallel.
They discuss Harmon's suspicions of Dena, her wealth
(the boat cost "ten grand" which indicates a "rich
daddy") rendering her indispensable but also suspect.
Josh doesn't allay these suspicions but simply say that
her continued direct participation is "part of the deal".
But that's exactly what Harmon is suspicious of: that
she's bought herself into an escapade whose demands
she may very well not be up to. Josh, a little surprisingly, seems at this point as close to relaxed as we've
ever seen him.

We are presumably now set up to expect the set
of permutations to be completed with the pairing of
Dena and Harmon (for ideal neatness they should be
discussing whether Josh is trustworthy), but we don't
get it yet. Instead we find the three of them sitting in
a restaurant, the arrangement of characters and camera
such that it's almost as if the film is trying to show
how difficult it is to show three people looking at each
other. The three of them are sitting around a small
table, Harmon facing Josh and Dena on the nearside of
the table, her back to the camera.

The painting on the wall (or is it a mural?) that
Dena is probably looking at is surely a reference to the
Lumière brothers' legendary film *L'arrivée d'un train en*

gare de La Ciotat, which everybody thinks was shown at the first ever public film screening at the Grand Café in Paris in 1895 (it wasn't actually first screened until the next year, in Lyon), and which audiences are supposed to have tried to jump out of the way of, although there's no reliable evidence that this ever actually happened.

I'm not at all sure what this reference is doing here. Why invoke the history of film and its ability to terrify, and to blur the boundary between reality and representation, at just this point? It would be far too obscure to see it as relating to the trio's difficulties with distinguishing reality from fantasy (something which concerns everyone who's ever made a plan, because it is in the very nature of a plan not to be real *yet*). It could be a joke about the film's failure to be a conventional thriller—an old film from the nineteenth century lasting less than a minute is more exciting!—but that doesn't work either, because at this stage the film is doing a very good job of being a gripping, albeit understated, thriller. Possibly something about timing is being suggested (the need for train timetables having prompted various developments in chronological standardisation), given that the trio's timing has already gone wrong: "I thought it opened earlier", says Harmon.

Josh is once again very tense after briefly having seemed relaxed with Harmon. (Does the presence of women in general make him uneasy, or is it Dena in particular?) I wonder also why it is Dena's face we can't see at the start of this scene. Certainly the patterning emphasises the gender arrangement of the trio. The Japanese critic Shiguéhiko Hasumi has talked about how it is simply *impossible* to film two people looking directly at one another: the shot/reverse-shot convention aims to disguise this fact. But the next shot (in which we can see all three faces) shows that it is, somehow, easier to show three people looking at one another than two. This underscores that the formal patterning of the three-way conversation in the trailer was a decision, not a necessity. Then again, it was necessary for it to be filmed the way it was in order to have the effect it does. The question of aesthetic necessity is a very difficult and delicate one!

Josh wants Dena to rehearse what she's going to say in order to be allowed to buy the fertilizer. His "I'm not worried about it" is so obviously untrue it's not even a lie; the relaxation we saw briefly has entirely departed. A member of the kitchen staff recognises Harmon; he doesn't even need to say "why don't you introduce me to your friends", doing it all with a look. Dena's humour (or perhaps better, her wit) is once again prominent: "how do you barely know him?" It turns out that the two men were in prison together. Harmon claims that he didn't mention it because it was so long ago that it doesn't matter, his record will be expunged by now. Dena has to lecture him about how the modern world works. Harmon might seem strangely naïve about this, but the unspoken accusation levelled by the other two is surely of recklessness rather than naivety, because of course he can't really think what he claims to think.

Another way of showing three faces is to have them *not* look at one another—as in the next shot of the three conspirators in the front seat of Harmon's truck as they arrive at the store to buy the fertiliser. I'll let you take the next scene—one of my favourites in the whole film.

Letter eleven

Dear Dom,

It's so interesting to read your thoughts on how Reichardt constructs a sense of unease in the conversations between this group of three, and the delicate balance between classic conventions and their being flagged as she builds up shot combinations. I'm especially enjoying the subtle changes in established relationships (such as the shorthand of Josh-Dena colliding with Josh-Harmon) as they start to dissipate and reform into other connections. As I was reading your letter, I kept thinking that certain aspects of the film seem to be directly concerned with Dena, as if it were *looking at her* quite often, which seemed one other way to read the café mural. As well as an image of the unstoppable approach / march of industrialisation (one of the key causes of climate change being given a 'seat' at the table), the train also seemed to be a pointing finger, a red flag about red flags. From the outset there have been more than a few moments—flaws in the plan, gaps in knowledge—which provided potential escape routes, occasions when a decision could (and maybe should) have been taken to reconsider, even to call everything off. Taking such offramps does not a thriller make (ignoring them does). So the train that may or not have caused cinemagoers to panic and leap out of the way (and it is not a *runaway* train but 'on track', the slow wreck for those-who-stick-with-a-plan-regardless…) is also a warning, facing Dena directly, urging her to get out while she can.

I was quite struck, too, by the establishing shot immediately before the café scene—another related scenic tableau of a family group *in preparation*, that could have been lifted from an 'outdoor' lifestyle / holiday brochure: a pair of canoes tied to a roof rack,

bright anoraks, studious children. A fleeting image, yes, but surely another nod to Reichardt's interest in planning, and indeed the 'wild' landscape being interacted with / commercialised, citing not only the visual language of what we're relentlessly being sold in terms of leisure and our relationship with nature. It's also a way to include walk-ons by bystanders, anonymous collateral. But it's no accident that it follows the moment in Harmon's trailer when Josh allows himself a luxuriant smile, talking about a shared acquaintance—a "lucky man" who has escaped back into the wild. This dubious wilderness lurks underneath much of the film, like a hidden reef.

Anyhow. The trio arrive at the feed store. We are in 'side mission' territory here, a standalone task that has its own internal logic, simultaneously low-grade setting and high stakes drama baked in. Dena is tasked with purchasing 500lbs ammonium nitrate fertilizer, even though buying more than ten sets off alarms for the authorities. The environment of the "feed store"—which I can only associate with large garden centres and trade DIY depots—takes us into the prosaic heart of the rural, smalltown setting and working community. From my own experience, there's usually something strained about going to these places (if you're an 'outsider')—they're riddled with clique, jargon, and ceremony, ranging from intimidating transactions, comedic exchanges, and absurd rigmarole, whether it be 'four candles' or something like my own Kafka-lite memory of buying a lump of turquoise in Mexico City—a marathon experience in which multiple chits, vouchers, stubs, and money, were traded, often more than once, with persons at multiple open counters and mysterious peepholes, until finally the brightly coloured brain-stone was handed over.

All that said, Dena seems calm and confident but she is difficult to read at this stage of the film. She vaults the low concrete wall like a military push 'over the top', having been primed once again by Harmon and Josh. It's not wholly clear why she has been nominated for this exposing task (did she volunteer?). Perhaps she is less known, both in terms of the local area and for previous activities; or they feel she can make the case more convincingly. Still, she's taking the biggest risk so far. Harmon's one-dimensional advice to keep to the central aisle (away from cameras) and not remove the hat raises questions as to how exactly he had been buying up the fertilizer until now—did he use the same tactic or frequent the same store (recalling the "Can I have twelve bottles of bleach, please?" routine in *Four Lions*)? It somehow makes more sense that they're 500lbs short. And does he presume that she will only need to visit the main shopping area? Or that she can stick with small bags of fertilizer?

In the store, the drifting focus of a following shot lifts the eye from obtuse codes and chemical specs on bags of powder to focus on Dena's back. Perhaps predictably, she immediately ramps things up, asking an assistant where she can find the bigger 50lb bags, aware of what they need but also abandoning the advice to go deeper into this overtly male environment. (By the way, I'm intrigued by the decision to have the assistant hold two huge ornamental bird baths in this exchange, one in each hand like oversized dumbbells! I like to think that Reichardt is ripping the piss out of the ripped…)

Redirected to the warehouse, with its shift in décor from a polished 'retail' to rustic 'trade', Dena is amongst a different set of codes: bulk sales, technical interaction, forklifts, and so on. Somewhere you are not meant to browse like a supermarket aisle. And the side mission enters another phase, with Reichardt relishing contrasts of light and shadow in setting up shots, embracing references both classic and cliché. The set piece turns into a Western duel, as we are introduced to a second assistant, this time rendered almost completely in shadow in the warehouse doorway: an anonymous gunslinger. Dena initially walks straight into the darkened warehouse, as we see and hear this gunslinger resolve a conversation with another customer. (And it is surely no coincidence that the 'triangle' of two men and a woman is re-established here, albeit briefly.) This is not only a clear hint of the familiarity of commerce here, where everyone knows each other, with shorthand awareness of anything outside routine: new faces, unusual amounts, etc. There is also, in a fragment of conversation just loud enough to discern—seemingly involving the gunslinger's incredulity that someone (a woman) thought a house "too small"—a faint but pointed intimation of small-town politics, power relations between the sexes, gender roles, familial expectations, and so on.

Dena comes into the darkness, close to the camera, and the gunslinger is silhouetted in the doorway. He is out of focus, faceless, with a lanky frame and languorous demeanour (somehow like Kramer or a neater version

of Old Joe from *Breaking Bad*). This must be a nod
to signature shots in John Ford's *The Searchers* (1956),
in spirit if not specifics, an image now so ubiquitous
and suffused throughout visual culture… It is such a
cinematic icon, in fact, that, given the reference to the
Lumière brothers earlier, one might wonder again
about Reichardt's motivation here. What's at stake, or
how far her tongue is in the cheek? I'm sure there is
a huge amount written on the cinematography of *The
Searchers* that I don't know about, but the instances
of the threshold silhouette in that movie do seem to
have different charges, currents, vectors… whether it
be the opening scene, when Martha Edwards (played
by Dorothy Jordan) is drawn out of the darkness of the
domestic interior into the brightness of the desert plain,
as wandering Ethan (John Wayne) comes into her orbit;
or the finale, when Ethan returns with Natalie Wood,
delivered like a parcel to the darkness of normality, but
himself remains on the threshold as the nomadic loner
who can never join the settled life inside.

One might say that in *Night Moves*, a similar
drama of being 'in or out' is actualised here. The bright
outdoor light—admittedly of a deeply unromantic
commercial yard rather than Monument Valley—is

framed by another threshold between wilderness and civilisation. It is also a portal between a 'dead end' and release, another appeal for our trio (or really, Dena) to get out while they can. The 'duel' also serves to emphasise Dena's isolation, as a young woman set apart not only here in this corral but set upon elsewhere too… The gunslinger seems calmly oppressive rather than threatening, standing between her and the outside. Yet the darkness contains no acceptance of a family welcome committee, so Dena ends up being pulled from pillar to post, living by her wits. Dena is pulled in toward the camera and rebounded out again. I'm conscious of overegging all this but there is something pleasing in conflating the experience of a woman buying fertilizer with a near mythic image of the American West, a portal between the homestead and wandering expansion… there's something else about rejection and renunciation here too, not just in relation to Dena's place in the trio, but also their collective and individual positioning against society (who need only be made 'to think', as Josh has it) and choices made in closing the door upon it. Still, the dialogue is where the duel takes place:

"Can I help you?" (A gunslinger's traditional opening gambit).

"I'm looking for ammonium nitrate fertilizer… Do you have that?" (She knows they do).

The "Did you look around?" reply is a sly dig, snarking about the fact that she has failed to adhere to etiquette and is browsing the backroom without his approval. Her neutral "A little" is met with further shit-housery: "Yeah? Nope, we don't have it." Ah, but Dena plays her earlier mistake against him with her "None at all?" (she knows they do) and manages to complete the stage, progressing to ask at the front office, in the belly of the beast. The comedic switch back to Josh and Harmon watching from the truck, as Dena unexpectedly walks from the warehouse to the office, is pure gold. We watch as they track her movement — slack jawed puppies, parsing eyes from a haunted painting — and it is both funny and oddly endearing. The shallow crescendo and slump of a whirring motor adds a dash of delicious slapstick too.

So, the Big Boss battle in the portacabin. Her adversary, beautifully played by James Le Gros, has the soft-eyed, friendly sheriff look, which chimes well with the ramshackle, inconsistently applied authority here. Her repeated enquiries are met with a straight-enough face, even though she seems callow again and undermined by glancing at a note. She populates the 10 acres with a range of produce, only adding the "goddam broccoli" at the end. It is interesting to me to note the script's absence of the one agricultural source mentioned Abbey's book: "…ammonium nitrate. That's powerful fertiliser, Doc. I got all we need at the watermelon ranch".* Big Boss offers an out by recommending sodium fertilizer as an alternative (less volatile but still potentially toxic to plants and soil in

---

* *The Monkey Wrench Gang*, p. 279.

high concentrations), compounded by the brilliant detail of calmly shooing a fly, demonstrating how he's going to bat Dena to the boundary. Him readying the paperwork, watching her ready the pen and ID, before adding the breathy "Social Security Card" is a cold, very late cut. Her surprised response is genuine here and his non-movement excuses a retreat to the truck. Harmon calls bullshit and reasons that to leave now would be more conspicuous, which is difficult to argue against, despite Josh being ready to split. More notable is the searching look between Dena and Josh (perhaps the last flare of their connection that we see) as they silently agree for her to go back in. The Big Boss watches the cap move up the office ramp (echoing the previous tracking shot), his expression hinting that he didn't expect her to return. Faced with her appeals, he doubles down. But Dena shows resolve too, probing as to whether there is any compromise at hand. Each time the negotiations run dry, where her nerve might start to fail or slip, she manages to revive the backstory, both digging a deeper hole and relaxing into the fiction. She becomes more believable the more she is pushed back. She gives specifics of distance (where does Pine Hollow come from?).

When it seems that he will not allow her to get *any* fertilizer without the card (and he arguably overplays here), she dispenses with the last seeming protection and removes her hat. This seemed to me another classic / cliché motif, of the seductress / femme fatale reasoning that she might emphasise her femininity to her advantage — 'collateral' being an hilarious euphemism here — despite the fact that she looks dishevelled, having slept in a boat / bomb (which may or may not have anything to do with the fact this doesn't have any effect). The glance to the security camera — which is confirmed with a cutaway to her POV, an anomalous use of this that underlies the peril (and indeed her awareness of it), compounded by a poised composition of cropped landscape image, caution sign (another one!), and a tower of disposable cups—again seems to spur her on for a last move. The sketch of the long winter pressurising production on the farm is an emotive upgrade, yet he still doesn't budge, so she again expands things to include dairy farming with 120 cows, which starts to rile him into movement as two older men come chuckling into the trailer. Seemingly without looking, Dena instantly grasps the chance to explicitly measure her experience as a citizen / consumer with that of others, and with the purchase point of implicit sexism, things start to shift. The pair entering the trailer no doubt echo Josh and Harmon waiting in the parking lot, neatly extending the comment on Dena's isolated role in this endeavour and a subtle indication of the invisible barriers she needs to negotiate just to play her part. Her last round is exasperated and inventive, citing an uncle, a named family farm (Nature's Harvest) and the fact that she gives a callback to Wilbur Milk is testament to the power of advertising with a dancing cow: "You probably drink our milk" is a precision strike and the jester's retort "If it's on sale" for some reason seems like the punchline that clinches it.

The fact is, Harmon might have been right or at least will claim to have been: a bluff was there to be called. We don't actually see the final acquiescence or transaction take place, and one wonders exactly how it gets resolved—not least the substantial question of getting 500lb of fertilizer into a truck without arousing further suspicion, either involving help / lifting machines, or driving the truck into some loading bay (a task that would presumably involve Josh and Harmon hiding or being clocked?), etc. There must be countless scenes in film and TV similar to this—the buying of controlled substances—but one that inexplicably sticks in my mind comes from the opening sequence of Michael Mann's *Heat* (1995), played out under credits. Val Kilmer's character is buying explosive charges needed for the next robbery—clearly a more explicitly dangerous controlled substance—under an assumed name, with false documentation, for a presumably fictitious construction company. Aside from Kilmer's puffy, nervous demeanour and a held stare when holding up an ID card, what there is in terms of tension is purely one way—nothing comes from the person dealing with the transaction, who remains entirely unconcerned. In fact, we have already watched him help carry the long wooden crates from outside storage to the counter, like he's part of the crew. It couldn't be a starker contrast to what happens with Dena.

One last thing. The sound design amplifies a buzzing fly at the end of the scene—not so easily shooed away!

Letter twelve

Dear David,

There are so many great ideas and observations here. Though inevitably I don't see everything in quite the same way. I'm intrigued by the idea of the train in the mural urging Dena to get out while she can, but I find I can't quite bring myself to buy it. For one thing, it's heading right *past* her, not at her. The risk of the march of history passing them by? But that kind of allegorical reading seems to be precisely not what the film wants to invite. (It's great that you flag up the establishing shot with the family next to their people-carrier; going back to it after the café scene, it too looks a bit like a mural, has something of the same kind of depth fitted into flatness.)

What you say about the sociology of the store makes me think that there are connections to be made with the final scene of the film, which hadn't occurred to me before, and to which we might return when we get there. The parallel you make with the legendary "inside-out" shots from *The Searchers* is fascinating.[*] The beginning of this sequence makes me think of horror rather than the Western, with the man (who of course we've already seen, but are unlikely to have paid much attention to, our focus being on Dena) looming behind her threateningly out of focus—but how interesting that both of us should read that sequence as an allusion to genre. There must be something further to conclude from that... I'm not quite sure, I must confess, I can see an allusion to *The Searchers*, but you're absolutely right that the man's stance is classic Western, which had never occurred to me before. Then

---

[*] I'm one of the people who's written (a tiny bit) about those images, he said immodestly, in *The Cinema of Disorientation* (Edinburgh University Press, 2020).

again, it can't quite be a duel because that requires some recognition of equality, which is precisely what he is (performatively) denying to her. But the age difference is important too, and he might well be just as suspicious of a baseball-hatted man of Dena's age. I wonder if you perhaps slightly overstate the level of his hostility? The man is certainly wary but after gauging her I don't think he's full-on hostile; he seems genuinely helpful about the front office. One of the things I really like about this whole sequence is how delicately balanced it is between registering the imbalances of power inherent in the relationships of gender and age that are involved, and revealing Dena's sensitivity to them. Which is not in the least to say that she's imagining them, but to say that what is important is their plausibility, their general possibility, as much as their specific reality in these particular encounters.

It's a great point about the film eliding the question of how to get the fertilizer into the truck. Points like this would have made the enterprise come a cropper if this were *The Mastermind*, Reichardt's latest film which I just saw yesterday. It's another film about crime and its aftermath, and it resonates (and often contrasts) with *Night Moves* at almost every moment.

On the question of why this job has to be Dena's — surely to a large extent it's because she's a woman? Which does indeed become crucial later; neither Josh nor Harmon could have got out of the pickle she gets into the way she does. The whole exchange makes explicit the importance of improvisation, which — or the absence of which — is one of the film's central themes, as we've already noted. Dena's decision to sit down and take up space is an inspired power move, forcing the discussion to prolong itself. But the — as you say — "femme fatale" gesture of taking off the cap and running her fingers through her hair just isn't going to cut any mustard, and the half-hearted way she does it shows that she knows it. Her mastery of the detail (which, combined with a bit of a sob story, is her next strategy) starts to get her on his side but would still have done nothing to change his mind had the two men not walked in at exactly the right time.

After all this verbal dexterity the film needs a bit of wordlessness. No words are spoken for more than the next five minutes. The buzzing fly transitions into the noise of a small cement mixer being repurposed as a bomb ingredient mixer. It's all sunlight and artificial colour (a bright blue groundsheet and still brighter yellow plastic bags). There's a bit more understated slapstick as Josh struggles to remove some of the seating from the cabin below decks. They load more things onto the boat, and then we see Josh dumping unneeded material at a tip, the woods behind ostentatiously beautiful in the slightly hazy sun. He visits a car wash and gets back to Harmon's place at dusk; the tip and the car wash were clearly, and prudently, not very "close". He climbs into the boat and inspect the explosives now packed into it. An unusual (for this film) low-angle close-up looks up at him as he nods with what seems typically self-conscious satisfaction. He approaches Harmon's truck with pizza but retreats when he hears the sounds of the two of them having sex. (Very nicely played: low in the sound mix without being coy; convincing but not really erotic in their effect on the film.) He wanders through the woods, the camera following beside him, showing him in right profile. He plays with a bit of grass and looks at his dirty hands.

The next morning, Harmon and Dena take a tarpaulin off a canoe and load it onto a trailer. Josh, out of focus in the background, is attaching the boat on its trailer to his pickup. Harmon passes Dena some rope to tie the canoe, his "will you go around and grab this" breaking the long stretch of wordlessness. Harmon tells Josh where he plans for them to launch the boat, then asks "You good with this?" He seems—albeit not entirely deliberately—to be asking at least three things: chiefly, whether Josh is happy with the general state of the scheme, but Harmon's interest seems to be more whether or not Josh has attached the boat to the pickup competently; and we might also wonder whether Josh hears a question as to whether he is OK with the changed nature of the relationship between Harmon and Dena.

Josh gingerly sets his pickup in motion—Harmon: "Easy! Heavy load!"—and they're off. Gentle nondiegetic music enters as the sun dapples the pile of explosives now packed into the cabin, the music's suspended quality sustaining the tension much more effectively than more obviously ominous music might have done. (There is also a comic cut to Harmon in his own pickup drumming his fingers on the steering wheel to metal.) It is dusk. A vertically arranged composition—river, row of trees, road, ridge, another road not visible but evident from the sporadic traffic—is held almost until the two vehicles disappear from sight. The film formally marks the transition to the next stage of the plan: this shot is one of departure, and the next is of arrival.

Letter thirteen

Dear Dom,

Although I think you're right to be wary about that reading of the train image, I'm not sure it matters too much that the train isn't heading *straight* at Dena, as it were, but sidling past. If the reference is to the Lumière Brothers' film and its (however apocryphal) effect on the audience, the conceit of Reichardt making Dena the cinemagoer in the shot arguably does enough work to associate her with the potential/necessity for evasive action. The train arriving at La Ciotat wasn't coming straight for the audience either (and similarly wasn't really there!) and still they were compelled to move... I wouldn't go out of my way to defend the perhaps over-enthused allusion to *The Searchers*, fun though it was—the nod to the Western is enough. The appeal to the gaming 'side mission' was also overegged, especially when it comes to the formality of the duel, rather than Dena sparring against different opponents, and as you rightly say, the theatrical equality is missing, as was the obvious reference to Dena's youth.

The sequences you've described also contain small details that relate to the intermingling of planning and improvisation, such as Dena using a saucepan to load the mixed chemicals into sacks during the wordless scenes of hard work. Perhaps it was your comment that made me see it, but I was also starting to circle back another rabbit hole since bringing up (and rewatching) *Heat*, as I wonder how much of a coincidence it is for both films to feature a fellow ex-con being recognised when working in a diner, and indeed whether any difference between them could be instructive? As we've seen, when this happens in *Night Moves*, it is passed over as an annoying but fleeting flaw in Harmon's backstory and his attitude to risk. In Mann's film, Robert De

Niro's sophisticated, super slick crew find themselves a man down, needing to improvise in order not to give up the impending bank job. The chance reunion with the disaffected guy working the grill leads to De Niro persuading him to join the gang on the spot, having little choice but to embrace the improvisation that is definitely not their MO. The guy is signed up as getaway driver, with fatal results. The notion of improvisation being the 'flaw' through which a plan can unravel, or at least change or transform, seems relevant enough to throw in the mix.

I wouldn't want to pass without comment the shot of the landfill site—"ostentatiously beautiful" is a great description—somehow like a cross between a truck advert and a balletic composition, with earthmovers moving in all directions and Josh flinging detritus into the environmental disaster zone like a shoegaze Merce Cunningham. I always find it fascinating to see exactly when a director decides to cut away from a long-held shot, and the explosion of white material that Josh tosses right at the end is choice farce, like office papers being jettisoned by The Crimson Permanent Assurance.

I wonder if there were more to say about the moment Josh walks into the woods alone (a stone's throw away from Harmon and Dena… in the Garden of Gethsemane…), as there seemed to be a particular resonance with what could be read as moments of doubt. It might be easy (for me) to misjudge the significance of the strange detail of him parsing the tree needle into two strands, then letting one drop, as if this were some hammy acknowledgement of Dena hooking up with Harmon, but there's also the lingering look (by him and us) at his hands. As well as an image of the day's labours, and perhaps a sense of things having been *imprinted* upon them all through their exertions so far—to the extent that there is *no way back now*—one also wonders if it serves as some strange, out-of-sequence image of guilt? Could it be a kind of pre-emptive hint of "Out, damned spot!" that is required to come before-the-fact as there will be no 'blood on the hands', as it were, given that fatal consequences will be held at a distance? The fact that Dena starts to itch and scratch in the truck, as soon as they leave Harmon's place, arguably indicates that Reichardt is indeed laying down first signs of what's in store for both characters…

The two vehicles arrive at Lake of the Woods together, pausing alongside each other at the entrance just long enough for Josh's uptight expectation of there being no one around to be countered by Harmon's missing-the-point ease: "This is nothing. You should see it in the on season." As they slowly coast through the campsite, the circling but off kilter soundtrack keeps up the undertone of tension. They pass parked SUVs and temporary encampments, fires and washing lines, families going about vacation activities and an underlying ring of children's voices, and Josh's demeanour is a complex mix of nervous self-awareness. He looks guilty, knowing perfectly well the risks they are taking, the absurd danger of pulling a huge bomb through this ephemeral, pop-up community. We get a clever interior shot, joining a shadowy couple sat looking out of their campervan windscreen, complete with dog on the dashboard and a small television screen suspended above them. The stacked 'screens' contrast the piped-in distraction of daytime TV from the potentially lethal drama rolling past the windows. The game-show contestant loudly winning just as a yielding quad-bike departs makes the scene seem choreographed, or blessed by chance.

We cut to a shot that has Josh and Dena preparing to launch the boat on a ramp in mid-distance. Reichardt

includes another anonymous family unit, this time a trio returning to camp after a long hike, drifting right-to-left through the foreground: Mother, Dad-on-phone, surly Teenager. The latter's complaint about how their "ankles are breaking"—to my ear overdubbed later on, a leavening addition to the script from post-production perhaps—offers another humorous reminder of the familiar and familial. Reichardt seems to enjoy mixing an emulsion of the deadly and the ridiculous, giving the whole thing a dressing of absurdity. A lingering shot of Dena, looking over her shoulder as the boat enters the lake, is striking, her narrow-eyed expression somehow cold and clinical. Yet we've had indications that this surface demeanour is not what it seems. Variations in their stoicism and their doubt continue to pile up when examined closely.

Launching the boat also seems to signal another significant phase in the plan. After a period of waiting that underlines their vulnerability—Josh, sitting in the boat alone, less anxious about time than whether the newly hooked up Dena and Harmon might abandon him?—all three reunite and cast off, dragging the silver canoe behind them.

On first viewing I really enjoyed the shots that follow, not least the first wide view of a patch of foreshore dotted with blackened tree stumps. It seems a fragment of landscape that is otherworldly, primeval somehow, yet the slick glint of the boat progresses in the distance. Two young boys play with orange pistols in the centre of the shot, improvising a game, it seems, that involves a relaxed violence, shooting rocks, all nature a target.

We cut to watching Harmon from behind, taking in the landscape as he pilots the boat. The strangeness of the surroundings bringing the soundtrack into distinct focus, elongating into elegiacally sustained chords. We move through stands of trees, this time stripped to bare trunks, flooded out at the root, felled on the shores too. As obvious consequences of the damming of the waters, these views become scenes of devastation, if not quite apocalyptic, stark enough to be reminiscent of photographs of the trenches in Flanders or the aftermath of an explosion. They are also quite beautiful as the camera arcs through them, with lens flares and crisp silhouettes, white clouds pressed onto deep blue. You could be reminded of Paul Nash paintings, such as the usefully titled *We Are Making a New World* (1918).*

* See https://www.iwm.org.uk/collections/item/object/20070.

Dena and Josh, hunkered down on one side of the boat, are attentive too. It feels that what they're observing is feeding their resolve. The damage they move through strengthens and nourishes their conviction, to the extent that nothing need be said. Any tone of sadness at the impact of the high waterline is fed into a sense of righteous determination. As if to emphasise this shift, Reichardt gives us a wider shot from the back of the boat so that we see all three characters together, and move with them through the flooded valley.

The spell of the sequence is broken by a dusk shot of the lake, churned by speedboats and jet skis, whose combined engine roar dissipates the music. The similarity to the sounds Josh was seen hearing back at the farm is emphasised as we watch him observe the pleasure seekers from the bank where the trio have stopped to eat. His expression carries disdain, as ever, but perhaps also a hint of vengeful purpose... They are closing in, arguably more determined and united than ever.

Letter fourteen

Dear David,

In saying I wasn't quite convinced of your reading of the mural and identification of an allusion to *The Searchers*, I very much hope I didn't seem dismissive. I certainly didn't mean that I was convinced of their wrongness—but, precisely, that I wasn't quite convinced of (or of the nature of) their rightness. My (qualified) identification with the tradition represented by the film writings of such as V.F. Perkins and Stanley Cavell make me interested in what Cavell calls, in *The World Viewed*, "humane criticism dealing with whole films", so I'm intrigued to see where these ideas fit into the pattern of the film as a whole.* (One pattern that I think we've touched on without raising it as a pattern involves children, small in the frame and intensely involved in activity: the ones you pointed out next to the people carrier outside the diner rhyme with the two with the orange pistols that you also highlight.) I'm certainly still puzzled and intrigued by the mural: I want there to be *something* more extensive in the film to do with early cinema, or the cinematic distance between now and then, at the very least, but I haven't found it yet. Eyes are peeled, but that's a difficult state to maintain when you don't really know what you're looking for!

Does *The Searchers* crop up elsewhere? I'm quite prepared to think that it may. Or John Ford more broadly? Questions of wilderness, isolation, civilisation, heroism, etc., very obviously invoke the Western but that, merely in and of itself, seems a bit thin. The geographical situation—Oregon—has, as in the later *First Cow*, a nice plausible deniability: we're very defi-

---

* Stanley Cavell, *The World Viewed: Reflections on the Ontology of Film (expanded Edition)* (Harvard University Press, 1979), p. 12.

nitely in the west, but not really the West. The pistol-wielding children might indicate both how the myth of the Western is, now more than ever, only a child's game—and yet also that *it still is* a child's game, its psychic pervasiveness has not entirely dissipated. It may be only a myth, but it's still *a myth*! Although, actually, the boys aren't obviously playing Cowboys and Indians, or even Cops and Robbers, but they appear to be shooting at rocks on the ground. Maybe playing with guns doesn't need a surrounding narrative pretext any more. And actually, the image of the sun through the trees that follows soon afterwards seems to me to invoke the iconography of the Western—rather neatly and ironically (given that we're in a flooded woodland) it makes me think of the desert and the parched hero stumbling around before collapsing. Is there a kind of split—what the characters are reading as encroaching environmental apocalypse we can (at least on a repeat viewing) also read as a premonition of their plan's disintegration and their impending isolation? Though I'm aware that I may very much be stretching things at this point.

Talking of patterns that run through the film, Josh looking at his grubby hands in the woods seems to be another instance of the film's tendency to play chicken with all-too-obvious metaphors. (See, particularly, the dying pregnant deer.) Here I'm reminded of the poet J.H. Prynne's aphorism that "clean hands do no worthwhile work", which I once found grounded and realistic but that now sounds like the kind of thing that could be offered to excuse any manner of sins.[*] (Trump will bring peace to the Middle East; it's self-indulgent to complain about all the other stuff.) The fact that, as you put it, "there will be no 'blood on the hands', as it were, given that fatal consequences will be held at a distance", surely emphasises the mendaciousness of any attempt to deny that the trio will, very much, have blood on their hands. I find myself wanting to say *literally*—when of course that's precisely what they don't have! But their relationship to what happens is precisely what that phrase *means*. So one wants to say "literally" as a way of emphasising reality, actuality. If you understand the metaphor you know that it applies directly to their situation. And in fact it does so much more precisely than saying that they are murderers (which is not quite right), nor manslaughterers (because there's no such word). (Incidentally, the best joke in the new Liam Neeson-fronted version of *The Naked Gun*—which is admittedly not saying very much—is him telling a man he's interrogating that his rap sheet says that he served 20 years for man's laughter.) The same kind of issue is present in Josh and Harmon's "I thought you said nobody would be here" / "this is nothing" exchange. Is Josh justified or naïve in taking "nobody" literally? In a less charged context Josh would be being pedantic at best. And yet of course

---

[*] J.H. Prynne, "Mental Ears and Poetic Work", *Chicago Review*, Vol. 55, No. 1 (Winter 2010), pp. 126-157, p. 141.

this is not such a context, and that does indeed change the meaning of things—but of everything?

Anyway, Cavell might say that with "blood on one's hands" we're dealing with an idiom, rather than a metaphor; see his "Aesthetic Problems of Modern Philosophy": "Someone might actually fall flat on his face, have a thorn in his side, a bee in his bonnet, a bug in his ear, or a fly in his ointment—even all at once." Whereas "to say that Juliet is the sun is not just to say something false; it is, at best, wildly false, and that is not being just false".* But then I wonder about the difference between a cinematic metaphor (the deer) and a cinematic invocation, or literalisation, of an idiom (to have got one's hands dirty). Both are connected to the idea of what a film *says*, or expresses, and resistance to them is—very properly—connected to resisting the idea that cinematic meaning is a matter of deciphering; that what films say is *coded* somehow. But perhaps one of the things that Reichardt is doing with these risky moments in her film is to resist, in turn, the idea that it's easy, or even possible, for films simply not to deal with that kind of meaning, as if they can short-circuit language entirely—something which, when claimed, is almost always presented as a superiority of film compared with the limitations of language. As if Walter Pater were right and film is at its best the closest it gets to the purity of music. Which might be a noble aspiration; Brakhage, maybe? Except that he seemed to aspire with his films as much to the condition of poetry as of music, as if film had to plunge back into language in order to escape or transcend it all over again. Perhaps Reichardt in the moments when she toys with idiom or metaphor or cliché is touching on the simple, but surprisingly elusive, notion that

---

* Stanley Cavell, *Must We Mean What We Say?* (Cambridge University Press, 1976), p. 80.

even though not everything is language, there's nothing we can't talk about. It would be intolerable for a film to consist of nothing but literalisations (a whole film of dying pregnant deer…), but to think that a film in which people talk to each other can just insulate itself from linguistic meaning as and when it wants could only be a self-deluding fantasy. Are the hints at visual metaphor themselves an indication that there's no such thing as clean hands—by which I mean some kind of "pure cinematic meaning"—where the interpretation of narrative cinema is concerned?

But these are probably pretty airy speculations, and I'm getting rather far off track, not to mention way ahead of myself. Since I might otherwise forget to say it, I wanted to note that the Paul Nash connection is interesting, and that Reichardt herself has Charles Burchfield's paintings as an important influence.[*] I love what you say about timing, or choreography, in that remarkably complex shot from the interior of the RV with its array of nested frames, by the way. An allegory for filmmaking, perhaps? (Since we've had idiom and metaphor we might as well add allegory to the pile.) Filmmaking as the art of arranging of contingency to appear premeditated, and premeditation to appear contingent. Which of course also allows for the double bluff, where the contingent really is contingent and the apparently premeditated really was. The shot from the RV very lightly rhymes (yet another literary term!) with a later shot from inside some kind of building (perhaps a visitor centre or canteen) with large horizontal widows allowing a panoramic view of the lake, and of Josh peering at the boat, making himself look suspicious. (Which in its turn rhymes back to the shot from the upstairs of the home of the man from whom

---

[*] See, for example, https://www.mattsmoviereviews.net/spot-light-interview-night-moves.html.

they bought the boat, in which Josh was the spyer rather than the spyee.) Of course there is no character looking out at Josh from the canteen whose gaze we are sharing. In a certain kind of thriller there might be, while in a better kind of thriller the point would be precisely to intimate the possibility without the film showing its hand. How well, and lightly, *Night Moves* handles this kind of thing indicates both how good Reichardt is at making a "proper" thriller when she wants to, and also why overly neat distinctions between plot and atmosphere are not to be trusted.

I love the cut to the lake with motorboats at jet skis—it makes a comparable joke as the cut to Harmon listening to metal in his truck. A kind of indecorous *parp* that undercuts the solemnity we had been led to share with the characters, reminding us that other people are experiencing this world differently. Though here it's less straightforwardly a joke, of course. But the humour serves as a bridge to the cameo of the chap (played by Lew Temple) who intrudes on the trio at their picnic table—Dena making peanut butter sandwiches—who you mentioned a while back, describing the scene as "a near-Wes-Anderson farce". The humour is explicit, if that's the right word. Harmon has just announced—crucially for the later development of the film—that after they split up later they shouldn't talk on the phone, which Josh enthusiastically endorses, repeating "no contact", the second time pointing earnestly at Dena. Dena repeats the same phrase. The rhythm of the splendidly chiastic dialogue—"Yeah, no contact. No contact!" "No contact." "Yeah."—is beautifully integrated in its flow. There is a beat. And then a voice offscreen chimes in: "Howdy!" He's perfectly judged in his utterly plausible affable goofiness, all nervous energy, bowlegs and bare calves. Quite sensibly—given how jarring any sustained *funny dialogue* might well have been—most of the humour comes from silence, as the camper's patter runs out in the face of resolute silence from the other three. The editing that keeps them utterly separated (apart from a single shot where we see the camper framed in the middle distance between Harmon and Josh) expresses the awkwardness perfectly. Our trio are *wishing he wasn't there*—and most of the time, as far as the image goes, he isn't; except that when he is, he's all that's there, egregiously intrusive. He gives up and leaves—"Take care!"—and after a moment Harmon gives Dena an absolutely perfect grin expressing the whole situation, while Josh yawns. Then suddenly, and quite unexpectedly, it's night and we're out on the water.

Letter fifteen

Dear Dom,

I certainly didn't think you were being dismissive and am keen to see how patterns play out too, self-conscious about not yet having a broader view of Reichardt's work (still a few films I haven't seen). I also can be seduced by details so a reminder to keep an eye out for wider patterns is always useful.

Although it might not yet be an echo that resounds into a wider pattern, I couldn't help but see (prompted by the still) the chirpy hiker as an inversion of the shadowy figure at the feed store. There's a similarly relaxed yet poised stance—hands at holster height—yet the hiker is presented in full light, explicitly upfront and unguarded, whereas the gunslinger was pointedly withdrawn and suspicious. We're not in a duel situation here, of course, yet it does seem like a deliberately staged encounter with another kind of *attendant* to the scheme at hand; a figure who is not necessarily trying to *stop* them but more like a gadfly from the everyday world, shadowing them like a (singular) Greek chorus that reminds them (and us) of 'ordinary' exchanges, collisions of mis/communication: friendly / strained, transparent / reticent, silent / verbose. I'm not sure where I'm going with this pairing / mirroring thing to be honest, but my feeling is that he's been written in for something more than comic relief.

At the same time, I was trying to figure out Harmon's direct, long-held, wordless stare at the hiker (which still seems somehow inexplicable, given that it has no effect! On anyone!) and then noted the character's opinion about his surroundings. "They fixed it up real nice" effectively puts him on the side of the dam builders, yet combined with his ironic reference to the "wild times" of the '80s (before the dam, one assumes?), we get another sense of ambivalence as to how people interpret their landscape, or what they as individuals stand to gain or lose through processes of change.

I agree that the motif of children is an interesting one and wonder if it's more than a hint at swings between innocence and naivety. In terms of the film's direct engagement with American myth, there is a 2013 interview in which the co-writer Jon Raymond casts *Night Moves* as a not-quite-pure embrace of the genre film (an approach that Reichardt elsewhere calls "degenerating" genre, which seems worth chasing up...). After Raymond cites Hitchcock and Noir, which obviously become more explicit as the film progresses (but could be earlier too?), he confirms that *Night Moves* grew "from a Western landscape and experience".* As well as Edward Abbey, he notes the books of Zane Grey and the Lone Ranger as reference points, notably foregrounding Josh as the 'outlaw' figure that occupies (or crucially *comes* to occupy over the full course of the film) an undecidable position of the individual both in and out of society. (One wonders what kinds of 'outlaw' Dena and Harmon are here?) I'm also curious to consider Reichardt's comment, in another interview, that "Westerns are made up of surprises, of moments that reveal" especially in relation to the slow shifts and 'hinges' we've already talked about in this film.†

What you write about the complexities of Reichardt's "playing chicken with all-too-obvious metaphors", filmic embodiments of moral commonplaces, even what it means for a film to *say* something, etc., is really fascinating and I am still unpacking it all. I suspect it will come back. I do find myself wondering, albeit

---

* Matthew Sorrento, 'Shades of Activism: Jon Raymond on *Night Moves*', *Film International*, issue 71, p. 124.
† Reichardt interviewed by Julien Bécourt, *Artpress*, issue 485, p. 30.

tentatively, whether it is useful to think of everyday language as a terrain; how such communication is shaped by those who inhabit it over time, through usage, an accumulation of habits and shortcuts, new and degraded images, literal and symbolic vistas, syntactical features, obsolescence, etc. To navigate such a landscape requires negotiation with all manner of byways and obstacles, from poetic grandeur to stupid junk, epic clichés and substitutions, monuments and monoliths, the readable and illegible... As much as a film and its characters might be said to grow from a given landscape, it also emerges from constructed language, a grammar of genre, etc. Hmm—not convincing myself as yet, but there's something in there somewhere. Still, if an idiom can be simultaneously literal and figurative, for the next few scenes at least it might as well be *in the same boat*...!

Back on the water, a pair of dock lights veers across the screen. The just-visible towed canoe orientates our movement in the deep darkness. This blast of urgency soon fades with the sound of the engine as the boat appears weirdly stationary again. We seem to be waiting before making the final approach toward the dam, involving some kind of specificity that we are not yet party to. The dialogue that follows is curiously subtle and complex. Shot within the confines of the boat—an open space effectively enclosed by the darkness—we are quickly aware of everyone's position in a three-way exchange during which only Dena and Harmon speak. At first the camera stays on Josh, silently impassive as Dena initiates a conversation with Harmon out of shot. If we are at first unsure as to whether Josh is listening, we soon become sure that he is. At different points, we see him wanting to be separate from any banal small talk but also aware that he hasn't been included. Without moving, he gives off aloof, needy, and judgemental fumes, sat in the crossfire of a conversation between two people who are themselves in a strange in-between state, both intimate and unfamiliar, having only just met and become lovers in quickstep. Dena's questions about the lake bring out Harmon's experiential knowledge. His enthusiasm for catching cutthroat trout further emphasises an embodied, pleasure-based relationship with the environment, a kind of worldliness (deserved or not) that starkly contrasts to Dena's. Her immediate recourse to abstract statistical health benefits of eating oily fish (with a notable mention of depression) is one that, if not quite *rehearsed*, seems connected to a programmatic ideological schtick that suffuses her outlook and use of language. His "all I know" response again stresses outdoorsman heroics, with practical knowledge preferable to book-learning, as if reluctant to look outside the fun of duelling with feisty fish. (Amusingly, I misheard Harmon adding "half-fish" at the end of a line, as if specifically identifying *himself* with the trout's capacity for resistance and breaking free… but I think it is: "I respect that… kinda fish"… Right?)

When Dena admits that she has never fished, she reroutes his surprise to an odd place: "I saw a lot of paintings of fish when I was a kid. Those were our family vacations, looking at paintings of places where we'd rather be". It is precisely this comment that moves Josh to look at her, switching his gaze with minimal movement, his eyes jumping like a needle on a measuring device. But what is he weighing up here? Does he tune in to wonder where she might go with this patter? Or acknowledge (for us) that he knows something of what she's *really* talking about? Or *wants* to talk about? If this is a hint at an unhappy upbringing, a tease of motivation, or a motif of belonging / escaping, might it shed yet more light / doubt on the shot of her looking at the mural (as if the train were an image of the means to get *elsewhere*)? More likely is that Josh here betrays his mistrust of Dena, sensing the unreliability in what she's saying (and we know her facility for fiction), that suggest doubts that may have origins before the beginning of the movie (despite his reluctant defence of her involvement with Harmon). With the smallest of gestures, she is cast as unstable. In the interview cited above, Raymond indicates that Dena was initially imagined as a "wild and unhinged person", always narrating and talking to fill space, yet this quality became muted through Fanning's performance.* How very slow cinema to kill off the character most guilty of potential exposition!

Dena's exchange with Harmon continues on its different plane (literally and figuratively). His chummy assertion that "someday you'll fish" offers a naïvely projected alternate future, and her explanation as to why this is not going to happen ("I'm not fishing now") revives her vaguely accelerationist doomy attitude to environmental collapse—for "It'll all go fast in the end" read "*It's already over*"—hinted at as far back as the film screening scene. It's actually an extremism that gets Josh looking at her again. At one point, I hear her saying "geometically worse", which seems weird. Is this a mispronunciation deliberately scripted (would "geometrically worse" make any more sense?) or left in as a naturalistic misspeak? Another sign of certitude being undercut? What I feel does get emphasised is a sense of (perceived) joylessness in Dena, despite her being the creative wit throughout, which makes her vulnerable to being judged for wanting to save the world without really having experienced it. Almost as a foil to his previous "all I know", Harmon's admiration—"You know a lot"—feeds Dena's lament for

---

* Sorrento, *op. cit.*, p. 125.

a wasted expensive education, again linking it to her removal from actual or authentic experience. Maybe one of the reasons why she is currently in this boat. Harmon seems genuinely disturbed by her responses and cannot help but revisit the wistful shared of going fishing "before it's all gone." He accepts her pessimism not so much in the language of romance but with a casual concern for her to experience and enjoy life more. She won't get much of a chance.

The deep contrast in lighting adds a beautiful abstract quality to the sequence that follows. The boat approaches the dam slowly, the top lit by a chain of inverted cones of security lighting. One might imagine patrolling *Wehrmacht* passing between these points yet the place seems abandoned—is this why they waited? Such a sabotage sequence comes weighted with tropes from war films and games aplenty, yet the film carries them lightly. The darkness adds a velvety slickness, the music tilts the jeopardy. The moment of contact with the dam is slow in coming, with characters silently setting themselves, trying to keep calm, as the tension builds toward a coordinated anti-climax. Josh uses his body to manoeuvre the boat along the curved wall as Dena hammers some kind of piton into the concrete with one blow—the minimum noise they can get away with—like a team of climbers given one chance to secure a foothold. As well there being no talk, it strikes me that the manoeuvre hasn't been rehearsed, at least as far as we know, despite it being something that could have easily been done badly. And it is again striking how the details from Abbey's novel have been adjusted. At one point in the novel the plan requires "three-four jumbo-size houseboats, the kind millionaires used, them sixty-five-footers", to be piloted toward the dam, before being scuttled at the appropriate distance, in order to "let them sink down toward the base of the dam, still moving forward under the water with the momentum so they come to rest against the cement".* Here things are more personal and hands-on, the placement of the bomb done with precision, with less left to chance. But then this gets flipped. Where the novel would have the next steps as: "we get ashore, we connect up the wire from all the houseboats to an electric blaster and we set off the charge [...] tamped by a million tonnes of water", Josh and co. appeal to the timed explosive, genre device par excellence.† As much as they don't feel the need to focus or maximise the explosive force through tamping (thereby risking greater collateral damage...), they seek to introduce distance. Our trio don't want to be there when it all goes off.

---

* *The Monkey Wrench Gang*, p. 159.
† *ibid.*

Letter sixteen

Dear David,

    I think that Harmon's line is actually "I respect that in a fish"; presumably there's a joke about whether he does or does not similarly respect human opponents who "like to fight". Is there regret here that they're not able to take on the enemy directly? Plus, I suspect, a hint of macho self-delusion. I'm totally with you on the resonances of stance between the shop assistant and the hiker; that's a very nice spot. There's probably a lot to say about posture in the film which I'm not sure we've touched on very much. Memo to self to keep an eye out for what happens to Josh's posture, in particular, as we move from the pre-heist to the post-heist portions. What you say about language as landscape also deserves having a marker put in it. Makes me think of this from Wittgenstein's *Investigations* (§18): "Our language can be regarded as an ancient city: a maze of little streets and squares, of old and new houses, of houses with extensions from various periods, and all this surrounded by a multitude of new suburbs with straight and regular streets and uniform houses". And "in the same boat" is great… speaking of developing patterns, the more we work through the film, the more I find I'm convincing myself that this awareness of cliché and its literal manifestation on film is a significant (albeit, I admit, probably not central) aspect of what the film is up to.

One more note before heading to the next bit of the film: I agree about the hammering-in of the piton not seeming rehearsed (though how *would* you practice it?), so just wanted explicitly to connect that to the dialectic of planning and improvisation that we've already highlighted. (Is that moment itself worth thinking about as another hinge?) Interestingly, when being interviewed about *The Mastermind* and comparing it to *Night Moves*, Reichardt said recently that "in the filmmaking part of it, you have a path to follow. You must get from here to here, and there's clarity in that. Then when you take that away, like post-heist or post-dam, the road is less clear and more improvising has to happen on the part of the character", and that the latter is "a different space to live in and to write in."[*] I take it that her point is that degenerating genre (degenreating???) is interesting precisely because of the nature of the move from the planning stage, which can only happen when there is a clear objective, to the improvisations that have to follow once the plan has been executed—and this on the part of the filmmakers just as much as the characters.

As the boat approaches the dam, do I detect just the merest hint of an allusion to the approach to the bridge in *Apocalypse Now*? Where that is a hellscape of noise, confusion, and red light, here the lights are cool and the quietness is palpable (despite the genre-appropriate music). But the tension is no less and there is a comparable sense of entering another world, of approaching a point of no return. If there is such an allusion, possibly it hints at the disorientation to come. I'm actually surprised how much music there is in this sequence. Given its status as the classic "extended wordless heist sequence"—see Jules Dassin's *Rififi* (1955) and Melville's *Le Circle Rouge* (1970) as the canonical instances—one would expect the silence here not to be cushioned by the film's score. Another instance, perhaps, of the way that Reichardt's supposed slow cinema associations get in the way of a clear view of what she's actually up to. Is the music here a misstep? I can't help but feel that the sequence would be even more tense without it, but

---

[*] See https://letterboxd.com/journal/kelly-reichardt-the-master-mind-interview/.

would that have been in a sense a little too easy? Or is it that it's particularly important to the film's purposes that it inhabits the world of the thriller—rather than the "art thriller", the kind of film your film buff friend *tells* you is a thriller but that is in fact just incredibly boring—as fully as it can at this juncture? (N.B. for clarity—I love "art thrillers"!) I think something like that is probably true, but saying it makes things feel calculated in the wrong way, as if a trick is being played on the audience, which I don't think is right. But then again, the disappointment some viewers felt indicates that some of them did feel that way. Though I don't suppose they'd really have felt it any the less had this sequence been music-free!

Anyway, the genre tension proceeds to reach its highpoint, at the exact midpoint of the film's duration. As the trio row the canoe away from the explosive-filled boat, a car stops on the road above, right next to the dam. There is a frequently repeated setup representing a literal point-of-view shot, the camera bobbing like the boat, that plays adroitly with abstraction, almost the entirety of the screen being jet black. For a while the film plays with the contrast between these shots and big close-ups of the three protagonists, looking up in wide-eyed tension almost exactly as if they're in a drive-through (row-through?) cinema.

Filmic conventions of the relationship between sound and vision are followed, as the dialogue ("yeah, it's right here") and the sounds of a tyre wrench and suchlike are unrealistically loud in terms of sheer volume, but plausible enough in terms of what the characters could probably just about make out. And then we appear to be about to get a bona-fide "defusing a bomb" sequence! The film's willingness to deploy "genre devices par excellence" moves closer to cliché, but the tension is very real. Harmon looks at the bomb and its timer with dejected tension. Does he know how to dismantle it? Is this something he's planned for? But then contingency avoids the need for improvisation, the car finally moves off, and the trio row away in a state of high nervous tension. I shouldn't, incidentally, overstate the generic aspects of this passage of play, as I've perhaps slightly facetiously been doing. Reichardt has spoken somewhere of how she actually shot close-ups of the tyre being changed, and little time-consuming mishaps (a wheel nut falling under the car) and even edited it together, Coen Brothers style, all the while knowing that it would destroy the narrative constraints that the film had set up for itself actually to use it. But how refreshing to have an excitingly tense bomb sequence with a timer that never gets lower than 11'18", rather than taking four minutes of screen time to get from 0'10" to 0'01"!

I'm impressed by the narrative and thematic economy of this sequence, as much as by the way it manages to be so gripping while avoiding both cheap tricks and hairshirt verisimilitude. It appears to be included simply for dramatic reasons—in the end the car drives away without incident and Harmon doesn't even start trying to take the bomb apart. And yet it also shows us that the trio were courageous enough to put themselves in genuine danger in order to avoid harming anyone. Of course this bit of bravery turns out to have been nowhere near sufficient; but it's probably important that at this stage in the film we share the trio's sense of relief in their triumph *over* contingency, *by means of* contingency. If that turned out to involve a bit of luck, well, don't things always? The fact that not everything can be planned for is, though, a jolly convenient excuse for not planning for something, and the impact of the film's second half requires, I suspect, that we forget this for a while.

Josh, Dena, and Harmon scramble onto the bank and push the canoe back onto the water to drift. The sequence ends with a beautifully anthropomorphic shot of the boat and the canoe, the latter tentatively approaching the former, both of them quietly expectant.

Letter seventeen

Dear Dom,

I confess that the first time I watched the scenes you've discussed, I had only thought that the trio were concerned about being spotted rather than the safety of the people in the broken-down car. I'm not sure what that says about me. Or indeed them. Still, you having pointed out the latter scenario adds further nuance to what comes next. I'd also initially thought that it was a police cruiser that had gotten a flat tyre in the exact right (wrong) spot—my eyebrows were raised pretty high at the filmmakers' *cojones* in having that happen before I realised my eyesight was worse than I thought. That *would* be too much… but just how far things could be pushed was clearly in my mind… In fact, I have since wondered about the needless, seemingly arbitrary imposition of the 30-minute countdown, which adds an urgency and pressure to the plan found nowhere else. There seems no concern for waiting to make sure the thing goes off (or indeed for fingerprints on boats, canoes, etc.—but I guess they get blasted to smithereens / washed away?) so why not an hour, why not two? The filmmakers' motivation seems clear enough—just enough time to be dramatic, for something to go wrong, for contingency to interfere. But what about in relation to the characters? Is it so they can be sure, as much as possible, that no one else is around to get hurt? Or minimum time needed to get to a safe distance without risking interference? I'm not sure. Clearly they have (had) a particular vision of how this is supposed to go down—another insistence on *idealism* being hammered home—and what happens doesn't match it. Of course, the point is that the setting of the bomb is irreversible in this case, something not factored in, and the called-for improvisation (aimed at stalling) is attempted but stalls. Harmon staring blankly at the detonator, like Linus with his blanket, is brilliantly pathetic—one wonders how long he would have sat there, surely knowing that he has no clue how to pause or disarm it? That's the true timer. As you've described so well, there's much to admire in this sequence in terms of how it plays against type.

Something here also resonates with what you say about the use of music in the sabotage sequence and its connection to a kind of romanticised aspect of scheming, foregrounded when the action is extreme: when ordinary people take on something usually encountered in cinema, is it inevitable that baked into their planning (indeed their sense of themselves) is a sense that it is all *as though they're in a movie*? And is it exactly this spell of genre that Reichardt is keen to accentuate and/to deconstruct? As well as being exceptional, extreme, the trio's actions are also genre clichés, seen a hundred times. As such, if the sequence had no music, might it be too realistic, too workaday, and not carry the same undertone of fantasy / genre delusion, and that it adds a necessary connotation of them only half in control of what they're doing…? Moves you make at night, as it were, are moves you don't know the extent of. Again, hmmm.

We cut to three shots of the trio running through the woods—with variations of framing that see them coming from behind, skimming over a camera on the forest floor, and panning right to left—but it is not quite clear how much distance they've travelled. What is clear is that they find the truck without difficulty. If this seems a little too easy, another genre-joke comes in to remind us: the truck doesn't start on Harmon's first try. In a moment that matches the bubble of the characters' incredulity, there's just enough space for the audience to think, *Oh, they're not going to do that are they?* before the engine starts up. Well, they're doing and not doing it, it turns out. It's a lightbulb moment too, as the dark cab comes to life. (This surely deliberate touch weirdly reminded me of the scene in *Close Encounters of the Third Kind*, after Richard Dreyfuss's car has been thoroughly *scanned* from above, sitting stone dead in the road after having gone haywire, when everything suddenly resets to 'original settings': engine and radio on, lights blasting, like someone emerging from a syncope as if nothing had happened...) As we've being saying in various ways, a lot of this has to do with the details of expectation—the meat and drink of genre and its degeneration. Reichardt's willingness to invoke these tropes is often so that she can quickly defuse them (rather than the bomb, to stick with literal and figurative fun!), as if the space of disillusionment that opens out is very much the substance of what she's after. As well as fatalistic deadpan humour, of course: *it would be now* when the engine won't start, wouldn't it, eyes rolling over in sockets oiled with fatalism and the inevitability of bad luck (for some reason an image of Basil Fawlty thrashing his red Mini with an oversized branch has popped into my head). She doesn't only thwart expectations but toys with them, thumbing the nose at genre catastrophism, picking apart the greeting card Lennonism: "Life is what happens to you when you're busy making other plans".

Once underway in the truck, as the sharp breathing of the trio's exertions starts to calm into silence, we come to arguably the most obvious hinge of the film: the offscreen explosion. Aside from the obvious practical reasons as to why the filmmakers wouldn't show the dam being destroyed, it is difficult to imagine it being done in any other way that wouldn't be inconsistent with the tone carefully established thus far. But it's only obvious in context. In fact, the scene is something

of an understated tour-de-force, not least in the way the sound of their being out-of-breath and full of adrenalin conducts proceedings. They are given time to quieten, as stares harden into introspective deadpans, all in a static shot of three people in a truck. It's clear that the drama and elation are short-lived. I find myself wondering how the exact timing of the explosion was decided upon in terms of their reactions. Was it left to the actors, or signalled by some marker, audible or otherwise? What happens when the sound occurs? We can trace a tentative smile in Josh but such expressions soon disappear. The nearest we get to triumphalism is a whoop from Harmon caught in the throat, the dour vibe sucking all oxygen out of it. He wants to talk but is quelled. Dena is particularly flat and featureless here. This is a crucial move, of course. To specify that this key moment—once the event we have been building toward has happened—is followed only by blankness and disillusionment. They might have gotten the same level of elation and satisfaction from nocturnal exercise. But I wonder if exactly this kind of disillusionment is the very substance of the film. Not only will the sense of achievement not last, it will be empty. And, as you have said, we move into a more dangerous landscape from here on in, where the teleological nature of the plan is no longer there to provide structure. Add to that the fact that plans don't fully deliver; plans do not resolve but sponsor other plans in their place. Now they need to improvise.

The trio drive to where the other truck is waiting in a forest parking area. As Josh gets rid of the tow hitch, there is an exchange of gazes between Dena and Harmon, the former seemingly dazed and in shock, the latter near biting his hand with rueful coyness. Clearly he thinks he cares for her more than he's let on, perhaps even seeing in her another kind of existence for himself. They're now to part, but it seems clear that this is not the last contact he would want with Dena…

There is a feeling of deflation as we come back to the truck pairing of Josh and Dena (Harmon's destabilising presence missed already?), as we also return to introspective silences familiar from previous journeys. Without delay, however, an emergency vehicle is heard. There is a brilliantly fortuitous reversal / misdirection whereby the red lights, reflected in the wet windscreen, give the impression that vehicle is behind them: could it be that the game's up and they're being tailed *already*?!

But no, it drives past them the other way, quickly followed by a second vehicle, this time observed from Josh and Dena's point of view: a one-two reminder of their plan's effect on the world. Dena shuts her eyes as the second one goes past. Josh feels moved to speak, yet his attempt at restating a plan only serves to underline how little there is of one—or how there *cannot* be one beyond "returning to work on Monday" and getting "back to normal" (instructions that are themselves ironic as normal behaviour is precisely what their actions were meant to stop). And normality doesn't possess anything like the kind of shape or potential for resolution as what has just happened.

As the truck moves crushingly slowly toward a blind bend, Josh tries to rouse a response from Dena, seemingly impatient to get her to acknowledge what he's said before the turn. In another subtle twist of farce comedy, her half-hearted acknowledgement (as if hearing him but not really listening) is then voided by a muttered "Shit" as the road swings around to reveal the bright tangle of a checkpoint roadblock. Are these the kind of 'reveals' Reichardt had in mind for her Westerns?

The haze of police lights might be another allusion to *Apocalypse Now* and there is a sense that things are happening too quickly just as they slow to a stop. Dena's scratching now becomes so pronounced that Josh notices, but neither of them lose their cool just yet. They wait in line and the police officer informs them they are checking the people passing through— no further details given. (What to make of the curious detail of the officer's torch only coming on—continuity error?—after she states she is from the Police Department? A strange callback to the light coming on when the truck started…? There is something brewing with the use of lights, as we know…) The exchange of IDs is notable for how long Josh looks at Dena's, as if worried she might hand over the wrong one, more and more conscious of her as a liability. He steps out of the truck and a close-up of his muddy boots emphasises how there *are* things to be noticed here, as well as underlining how recently, and how nearby, they have done the deed. On first viewing, of course, we're not sure how thoroughly they've gotten rid of any evidence, or what kind of incriminating material might be left in the truck. The tension released by the tight, torchlit reveal of the vegetable box is satisfyingly basic. Josh, perhaps fumbling to reawaken the skill of talking to people outside the 'cell' of their scheme, starts to explain the Community Supported Agriculture deliveries without being asked: a pleasing switch from secrecy to outreach programme!

The scene ends with the police officer moving to the next car, the occupants another male / female pair, not dissimilar in age. It stresses their un-exceptionality and perhaps suggests that Josh and Dena might blend in, and that, having gotten though the checkpoint, they might just get away with it.

Letter eighteen

Dear David,

Just one more point about the music here: its presence as the three of them set the bomb makes its absence as they run breathily through the woods, and all through the ensuing scenes that you've just described, all the more effective. The music comes back again over a brief shot. It's still night-time and still taken from a moving vehicle, but now looking up at a deep blue sky above trees, echoing in some ways the views from the car on the way to and from the hot springs that are one of *Old Joy*'s distinctive stylistic features. There's a peacefulness here, but it's not clear whose.

And then it's daytime and the camera pans very slowly right across what turns out to be Josh's bedroom, I think some kind of yurt constructed out of a wooden frame making lozenge shapes and an outer skin of material. Though we don't know this immediately; things are, again, quiet and peaceful but it's hard to tell where we are. There's a very different cinematic grammar here from the preceding action scenes, not just because things have slowed down and quietened down but because we don't know whose point of view we're seeing. Literally, it's that of nobody in the film world, but the moving camera I think reemphasises the sense of the film's point of view, something that the tension of the preceding sequences didn't give us a great deal of time to ponder. The movement of the camera insists on the idea of *direction*, of there being somewhere we're going, but where that is is almost entirely opaque.

Eventually the camera reveals Josh lying on his bed. We can see his face but the medium long shot makes it hard to see in detail. Presumably, he's thinking about what he has done. But in what sense, I wonder? About its consequences or implications, or about *what* he has done, as in—how best to describe what they did? Then the shot with the ambiguous point of view is succeeded by a literal point of view shot. Josh is looking up at the featureless circle of sky through the hole at the top of the yurt. The metaphor alert goes off again: an unreachable point of escape? But when we cut to a close-up he looks unexpectedly happy (indeed self-satisfied) and, actually, rather post-coital, an impression that is heightened by a cut to him putting on his trousers. Maps, papers, and pamphlets cover the floor at his feet: evidence of preparation for what is now completed? (Although presumably Josh considers them un-incriminating enough not to have destroyed them.)

He slopes off in his characteristically round-shouldered way through sloping countryside to the communal building. The other members of the communal farm are discussing the dam that was blown up the night before. In a very nice touch, it's causing neither consternation nor exhilaration but a bit of laughter and an opportunity for a bit of teasing. ("You wouldn't have the organisation skills to pull of something like that!", one of the young women teases one of the young men.) It's a diversion over breakfast. Reichardt adroitly introduces the crucial plot point that a man who was camping downstream from the dam has disappeared. The slopes from the previous scene are recontextualised—a younger boy jokes, "I am never going camping again—well, unless I'm uphill!" Josh is seen in close-up, the camera gently pushing in (Reichardt unafraid of a very familiar device, and rightly so, because it serves its purpose while remaining unobtrusive) and a discussion of ethics and effectiveness goes on in the background ("my sympathy's with the water on this one"). The scene serves as a Brenez-style fold or pleat, connecting back to the discussion about environmental activism at the film screening in the first part of the film. Sean admits that whoever blew up the dam has a "point", but destroying one dam won't make a damn bit of difference. (Sorry about that; I think that's one each so we can stop now.)

Katherine Waterston's Anne, who thinks that Josh has been out in Portland tells him that it "looks like you had a good time", again underlining the sexual structure of the event, its climax and present aftermath. Waking up after the night before. We then see Josh at work on the farm. I very much like the fact that there's not a more abrupt "culture shock" at being thrust back into normal life, which I think would have been the obvious choice. A car behind him reminds him—and us—of the car with the flat that made them try and defuse the bomb. Then, working on vegetables in a kind of polytunnel, the sound of another vehicle makes him briefly turn off a large fan so as to hear better. Josh approaches the camera suspiciously.

There follows a paranoid point of view shot through the opening of the polytunnel: another echo of his looking down on Dena from the first floor of the house of the guy they bought the boat from. Then, immediately, yet another rhyme: the young woman, who the credits tell us is called Surprise (Alia Shawkat) is operating a cement mixer. Presumably, just like the last one we saw, this one is mixing fertiliser—although I'm sure this time it's wholly organic. I'm starting to wonder whether most things in the second half of the film have their pre-echo in the first half.

There's another group scene, this one happening outside. Surprise is showing a boy called Felix how to douse, both hippie and sarcastic: "That means you're spiritual" / Your aura level just went down". Is there another metaphor lurking here? Will Josh be found out, no matter what? Even if he left no material evidence, the aura of his crime will somehow give him away? Although I then realise I've slightly misinterpreted: it's not dowsing as such—it's an "aura reader" that she's constructed, two sticks attached to a wooden backpack, Ghostbusters proton pack-style. I'm not quite sure how to take her intention here: does she think it's simply a toy, or is she pretending that this is what she thinks to cover any embarrassment at taking it seriously? Maybe I've spent too much time in Josh's company: she takes it entirely seriously, which doesn't prevent it also being fun. At any rate, it allows the film to include the line, delivered by Surprise rather softly in the background, "now it's time to see who you people really are".

Corser (Barry Del Sherman) sits down next to Josh. He has "burned" his "cheese license". The FDA "knows", but he "hasn't heard a word". He's a different kind of criminal awaiting detection, but Josh doesn't seem to recognise the parallel; it's more of a relief to be thinking of somebody else's problems. His phone rings and Josh walks away to take the call. It's Harmon, worried about Dena. We realise that the focus has all been on Josh for the past few minutes. Perhaps even feel a bit of guilt for not thinking about the other two? Although this may just be me. The shot that you discussed of the three of them in the truck, in which we hear the dam explode, is terrific in how it shows both their togetherness and their isolation. They're three people sitting next to each other, but are they a group of three or are they already, at that point, something else? Both the framing and lighting I think suggest Dena as the protagonist, as the focus of attention, a shift in the film that would be entirely plausible. Possibly we're even meant to slightly regret that this didn't happen: the sense that, in spending so much time with Josh, we're stuck with the one of the three we would be least likely to have chosen may be another reason for the frustration some viewers feel about the film—though the effects of shifting Dena offstage at this point strike me as one of its deftest achievements.

Josh is both disappointed and annoyed that Dena has "been calling" Harmon, not him. Even though of course none of them should be speaking at all. (Shades of *The Big Lebowski*'s Walter (John Goodman): "Erev Shabbos. I can't drive. I'm not even supposed to pick up the phone, unless it's an emergency." The Dude (Jeff

Bridges): "It is a fucking emergency." Walter: "I understand. That's why I picked up the phone.") "She's not doing so good," Harmon tells Josh. He asks what this means, repeating the phrase. Josh wonders whether Dena would "do anything stupid": he *wants* to mean "kill herself", but he really means "turn herself in". The hint at tears as Josh eventually comes round to asking how Harmon is doing are brilliant in how much they encompass. I think I see something of the self-pity that is such an important part of Josh's character here: at some level perhaps they register his recognition that it's only himself that he's really worried about, when it should be Dena. But the near-tears also express the sheer relief of one kind of tension even as another sets in, as well as the feeling of lostness now that the plan has been executed. In more senses than one, they hadn't planned for this.

Letter nineteen

Dear Dom,

　　We might have to add to the pile of things to look out for—alongside hinges, mirrors, echoes—the various spiral motifs and nods to circularity. As well as Josh's living space (a bubble, I daresay), the way the camera spins into him and indeed the round hole in the roof of the yurt, I was reminded of other spinning objects, whether it be the cement mixer (especially when we cut to a closeup) or the 'drill bit' windchime that appeared at Harmon's place (just prior to Dena and Harmon screwing!) and which I think recurs later at the spa… Points of escape, yes, but maybe also traces of insularity and premonitions of the inevitable. I think you're right about characters other than Josh being shifted slightly to the side from here on in, as part of the deftness is how it heightens the sense of claustrophobia that would be punctured if we were to get a breather spending time with another character. From the outset of the aftermath, though, it seems that Harmon is in another category still, relegated to a voice but there until the end, taking on the role of someone just as implicated but free enough to act as devil on shoulder / reality checker: "But it's happening." Given his strangely disembodied role, I find myself intrigued by the abruptness to the way that Harmon hangs up the phone on Josh. It could be him being his casual self, miffed at the belated inquiry as to how he is doing. The "I'm OK" seems assured but the subsequent "sure" does something else. More than that though, there seems to me to be an accelerant in the way Harmon sets up what's happening with Dena and the subtle gaps of implication he leaves as to how it should be 'handled'. I might be way off, but the way the silence is skewered by the sound of the call ending is particularly pointed. My feeling too is that Josh desperately wants to talk, perhaps even as much Dena, although he could never admit to this. His searching eye movements and the near-tears you highlight nonetheless suggest as much. And so, the way Harmon leaves him hanging adds extra weight to what he has to do: confront Dena alone and in-person. The non-communication pact has already been broken, but he doesn't call her. She's been assigned as *his* problem and one that requires additional measures.

Music emerges at the end of the phone call scene, as we cut to another night journey shot from a moving vehicle. As well as echoing the other window shot, the film sets up another action sequence, another task (another defusing). The night moves emphasise distance travelled, and efforts made, underlining how deliberate a move it is to go to Dena in person. It seems late to point this out, but it is striking how often in this film we're given a view framed by a vehicle, looking both in and out. But this road-bound sequence seems different, less a character's point of view than that of the truck itself (I guess I'm being prompted here by your comments re: the yurt spiral). I'm not quite sure if there's something here or not. I have in my mind something vague about Chris Petit's *Radio On* (1979) consciously embracing the cinematic nature of the windscreen view, complete with drama streaking by and a built-in stereo soundtrack, but where that motif might still place us within, or include elements of, the truck interior—steering wheel, dashboard, character, etc.—here we have a strangely disembodied view, as if separated from any specific scaffold, and the headlights become detached viewpoints, mechanisms of a mobile gaze… urgh.

In a dusk-lit scene, we see Dena finishing work at the spa, saying goodbye to a colleague and starting to walk home. If we can judge things on this passing moment, everything *seems* normal—at least we see she has stuck to the plan of returning to routine. Dena wears the white cardigan, which makes her sharply visible in the darkness, especially when highlighted by streetlights. As a colour in stark contrast to her outfits from recent night scenes (which might have been quite Josh-like, in fact?), one wonders if there is an intent here to visually emphasise change in Dena here, whether it be toward a renewed moral standpoint or resolve, to signify accountability, regret, shame (even an attempt to reclaim innocence?)—the key point being that most of these possibilities might be seen as the preliminary stages of confession. In any case, the camera pans slowly with Dena then, when she is perpendicular to the camera, a repeated flash of headlights confirms that we have been watching her from Josh's truck parked across the road. It seems almost melodramatic but we're in territory that owes a debt to noir stakeouts and such, and both characters *know this*. The timing of the light salvo is precise—another planned operation here—and results in Dena being symmetrically framed by the roadway behind her, an alignment that empha- sises how she is now the focus, literally and figuratively caught in the headlights and targeted. The cinematog- raphy casts her as particularly vulnerable on the street too, which actually links up with me only just noticing that in the blurb about the film her character is desig- nated as "runaway".

We don't really register her recognition of Josh being in the truck but she moves to cross the road, perhaps wary but without obvious resistance. She remains on the threshold, however, just inside the truck door, offering a slightly different take on their agreement: "I thought we were going to stay away for a while", a tentative shift of blame swallowed up by what

is to come. She is evidently reluctant to get in the truck and Josh's overcooked "Come on in" seems to emphasise his position of power and control in the scenario. Having Dena shivering with cold here is a great touch, making the sense of her caution and anxiety (as well as suffering) palpable yet explicable and at-a-distance. Once she is in the cab, the lighting allows us to see the significantly larger area of rash on her face and neck, lending her an air of illness and vulnerability. In fact, I was reminded of Edvard Munch's series of drawings, prints, and paintings on the theme of the 'Sick Child', related to his sister's death from tuberculosis; complete with profile view, gaunt face and fever-damp hair.

Once her communication with Harmon is established, Josh starts to lose control. Her level of anguish is not something Josh has planned for. His appeal to generic 'worry', even 'natural' upset, is not only insufficient but sends him spiralling. It's soon clear that he doesn't know how to play this. If there was a sense that Josh intended to even tacitly strongarm her, to come in like the stable adult to calm the waters, his lack of genuine sympathy undercuts him. Even his wanting to know if she wants to talk rings hollow.

As she so often does, Dena ratchets things up by asking if he has seen the website. His too-quick answer does a few things, perhaps initially betraying his terror that she has already made something about what they have done available to the public! It also doubles as a giveaway as to his disengagement from the 'grid'—*of course* he wouldn't be online to hear about it—which triples as a sign of his disengagement with consequence, which for Dena is tantamount to not caring. One feels a slight twinge of sympathy for Josh's clumsiness here, as him not being fully up-to-date with the news of the missing camper doesn't fully equate to a callous or uncaring attitude. But at the same time, his wounded response to her comment is a bit much. If he hasn't seen the website, it is clearly something Dena has been looking at, torturing herself with comments from the missing camper's friends and family. Josh tries to hold on to the lack of confirmation as long as he can.

Dena's disbelief about the situation—"I can't believe this"—prompts a long stare from Josh. He seems tired and his look has a red-eyed, menacing quality. Here, perhaps, Josh gets closer to understanding the seriousness of her situation, so he subtly changes tack: his delivery of the phrase "not what anyone wanted" is particularly patronising and creepy, simultaneously accepting blame and foregrounding denial. It works only to get Dena shifting blame onto Josh, as if the parameters of the whole scheme were determined by him: "You said no one would get hurt. But they did." As well as a naïve disavowal of her own complicity it also introduces an instance of the plan having an alternative form, where they could have done it in the winter season instead. As well as being another deft move by Reichardt to offer concrete options after the fact—we also circle back to the literal/figurative discussion in the citation of "no one" being around. This time Dena seems to believe that if only it had been done *that way*, not only would the camper not be missing, all risk would have been eliminated. Josh responds to this shift in tone with more aggression and scorn: His "What did you think was going to happen?" twists away from its echo in his own prior conversation about the cheese licence, perhaps suggesting that however you project toward the past or present, whatever your starting point, something of the outcome will remain unknowable.

There's an interesting play between vagueness and specificity in all this, especially when Josh leans in: "What are you going to do? Are you going to *do* anything?" In being very particular about such a non-specific action, the tacit understanding is all the more threatening. Dena picks up on it and challenges him: "Is that why you're here?" The specifics of the reasons she offers—that she might call the cops or contact the Halter family—no doubt confirm for Josh exactly what he fears she *had* considered doing and, coupled with a vague "I don't know" when exiting the truck, brings things to a head. Josh grabs her wrist and stops her. A plan-less move. He responds with some shock at his own actions when Dena says he is hurting her, and the whole scheme of things seems tragic and haunting here. There is a desperation in both of them now. Josh is left alone in the truck, unable to control the situation, or himself. If he is clearer about anything, it has to be that he has made things worse.

We cut to a bright morning scene on the farm with a row of people sorting vegetables. The dam explosion is still the subject of conversation yet when Surprise sees Josh approaching, she baldly changes the subject. The boy she has been joshing with (sorry) knows the reason too. Surprise surprise, *everyone* seems to know. In an even earlier scene, in which Josh and Sean silently lay protective fabric over a vegetable patch, it is made clear that Josh is instantly under suspicion, so obviously in fact that his boss seems convinced of his involvement. It's already over bar the confirmation.

The next scene sees Josh climbing the steps of the Public Library later that morning. Being unable to hear the librarian's refusal (an oblique echo of him turning off the fan in the earlier scene) gets him a foot in the door. The soundtrack returns, adding to the atmosphere of portent in the abandoned reading room and ramping up the suspense of Josh's minor break of cover. He heads straight to a computer and gets online, seemingly not seeking the website Dena has mentioned or perhaps having this be superseded by a local news page. The missing camper, Bill Halter, has been found drowned some miles downriver. In a partially obscured close up we watch Josh's parsing eyes confirm all that he had been trying to deny. Although it is after the fact, it is the closest we might get to Josh being "[h]eart shocked to a stop, brain blanked dead", as Hayduke is described in *The Monkey Wrench Gang* when he sees an engineer on the supposedly automated train they're about to blow up.* Still clear-thinking enough

---

* *The Monkey Wrench Gang*, p. 201.

to delete his browsing history, Josh turns the computer off and gets up from his chair. Low down behind him, the camera rises too, but continues to rise into an obviously disembodied, somehow *structural* position above him. Structural is not the right word but there is something being built—does it relate to the disembodied headlights from before? We haven't quite had a shot quite like this, and the effect is striking—both slightly contrived and very effective. Josh gets pinned down here in the looming composition, which surely echoes the height of the floodwaters detailed in the online article. It might be a hinge, it might be an explosion. Belittled and under pressure like never before, Josh puts his hand to his face, a bit like Harmon when saying goodbye to Dena. We tower over him as he wanders to a stop amid a distinctly watery carpet. He is a different kind of adrift now and there's no denying it.

Letter twenty

Dear David,

The sense of lostness and threat that Josh is feeling (adrift, as you say, or even "all at sea", to return to our earlier thoughts about literalising metaphors) is sustained across a transition to a completely different kind of image. We're at a produce market and a surreally still camera and equally surreal slow motion, coupled with what, in comparison to the library, feel like un-naturalistically heightened colours, convey Josh's sense of vulnerability and isolation. Everybody seems to be looking at him, an impression which the film generates via the supposedly taboo (but actually pretty common) device of looking directly into the camera: a woman holding flowers; a policeman; a young man with a bandana, a drum on his back and a kitten on his shoulder.

The kitten's excessive cuteness contributes very nicely to the Lynchian dislocation going on here. There's a connection to the mood at the beginning of *Blue Velvet*, waving firemen and all, although there the effect is directed towards the sense of what is concealed by the too-cheerful, too-brightly-lit surface, whereas here there is something more centripetal going on (there's that circularity again). Josh is threatened simply by being at the centre of his world in the way that all of us are always at the centre of our worlds. The music oscillates ominously and then the sound abruptly becomes "normal", as Josh surfaces from his reveries. However, the phone conversation we then start hearing (between Josh and Harmon) isn't taking place in the bright daylight during which we begin to hear it but later, at night. Introducing sound from the next scene before the image changes is an ordinary cinematic convention but here, given that we have no reason to think that the conversation *isn't* happening simultaneously with the image of the market in daylight, rather than bridging scenes smoothly, the device only adds to the sense of dislocation.

Harmon tells Josh that it is "just a matter of time" before Dena talks. Coupled with other remarks, such as that "jail don't sound so good to me", we're prompted to wonder what kind of speech act is being committed here. Is it an instruction to Josh to do something about the situation? Despite containing plenty of wordless stretches, this whole section of the film is deeply interested in what we achieve by our words; or, perhaps better, in the difference between what we literally say and what we actually say. For example, I think I'd disagree that Dena's earlier "I can't believe this" (to Josh in his truck) expresses *disbelief*. She doesn't mean that she is having trouble accepting a piece of evidence, but rather that she's distraught by what is going on, would prefer it not to be happening, and is daunted by the action it's going to require of her. (Which is of course very often what this phrase means—see Victor Meldrew's favourite variation on Dena's line as a notable case in point.) Similarly, Josh's "What did you think was going to happen?" is an admonition, not really a question at all. (Which is not to say that Dena couldn't have supplied a genuinely informative answer to it.) Your spot of the way that this line echoes the cheese license conversation earlier is very good. There, the question was "What do you think'll happen?" What strikes me about the relationship between the two questions is that the second question is *not* just asking the same as the first, but now about a prior mental state of Dena's rather than about what is going on at the time the question is asked. The way a simple change of tense changes the whole function of an utterance has quite profound connections with the film's interest in the passage of time and the irretrievability of our actions. What is different about the past isn't simply that it has already happened; there are deeper and more complicated transitions at work.

These issues of time and responsibility are interestingly mapped by the film onto questions of activity and passivity. I really like how you pick up on Dena's shivering. (Though I don't think it's only cold that she's shivering with.) The way the shivering relates to what is being accomplished in the conversation between Josh and Dena is illuminated by some remarks of Elizabeth Anscombe's about the relationship between voluntary action, following an order, and being the consequence of something spoken:

> "A voluntary action can be commanded. If someone says 'Tremble' and I tremble I am not *obeying* him—even if I tremble because he said it in a terrible voice. To play it as obedience would be a kind of sophisticated joke (characteristic of the Marx Brothers) which might be called 'playing language games wrong'."*

---

* G.E.M. Anscombe, *Intention* (Harvard University Press, 1957 [2000]), §20 (p. 33).

Dena's shivering, or trembling (it's quite interesting how it affects one's viewing of the scene depending on which word one primarily bears in mind) is a particularly good touch because it puts Dena's skin rash on a kind of sliding scale of involuntary physical actions. One might have felt that the rash was a bit of an overstatement by the film: she's not just feeling nervous and guilty, her guilt is *manifesting physically*! But I think by relating it to the shiver we can see the rash more as something happening *to* Dena—a *reaction* as opposed to a *response*—and so as part of the whole context in which she has to decide *how* to respond. It's true that all this brings up ideas of, as you put it, "accountability, regret, shame", which "might be seen as the preliminary stages of confession". I also think that there is a link, rather than a disparity, between Dena and Josh here in that she too, seems (I think probably contrary to what she would have expected) conspicuously self-interested. She hasn't really rejudged their actions, she just doesn't like how she feels having done them. She would like to have done the same thing but at a different time of year—but had they done that, they wouldn't have done *the same thing*. Her reproach that "You said no one would get hurt. But they did." is, I suppose, "a naïve disavowal", but of course she also knows this (just as they know that they're in noir territory, as you point out). It's a form of childishness—and of course, with her money and background we are, I take it, to assume that she was what we used to call a "spoilt" child. (I don't think her remarks on the boat have to be seen as challenging this; spoilt children are often unhappy.) She even looks younger during this scene; the white cardigan helps; but she also seems *smaller* somehow when sat in Josh's truck. There is petulance from both Josh and Dena, indicating a parallel between them just when she seems (and, indeed, is) the more admirable. This is the kind of subtlety that I think Reich-ardt really excels at. As I said, it's not that Dena *isn't* the more morally admirable here (this isn't a "you can never really judge anyone" relativism), but it's that it's a wonderful touch to display resonance between the two characters at just the moment when a lesser film would set them off more emphatically by, say, presenting in Dena a nobility that Josh is incapable of.

Much of the formal work at this point in the film serves to set up a different kind of parallel between Josh and Dena, one that emphasises the difference of their positions. After talking to Harmon, a horizontally tracking camera follows Josh walking through suburbia at dusk. The figuration is a reversal of that in which Josh tracked Dena, which you pointed out; this time the camera's point of view is the threatened person, not the threatener. (When Dena walks slowly towards Josh's truck, and hence directly towards the camera, it strikes me as reminiscent of *It Follows*—which of course came out a year after *Night Moves*—but with the threat behind the camera instead of in front of it.) Whereas in the earlier sequence the tracking shot repre-sented Josh's point-of-view, here the subsequent shot is from his POV, showing Dena at home in an upstairs window with somebody else (perhaps her mother). This is also formally a variation on the market scene and its portrayal of surveillance; here Dena doesn't know that anyone is looking at her, whereas earlier, of course, nobody *was* looking at Josh in the way he felt they were.

There's a sense in which this part of the film is rather like Hitchcock's *Shadow of a Doubt* (1943) but with Joseph Cotten's murderer, rather than his young niece, as the central consciousness. The dread of exposure is central, rather than the moral imperative to expose. (Think how utterly different *Night Moves* would

be if Dena were the central consciousness at this stage.) The film makes the link via a direct citation. Both films contain a nervy trip to the library; here Josh arrives before it opens, whereas in the Hitchcock, Charlie (Teresa Wright) arrives after it has closed. The two librarians have exactly corresponding dialogue: Charlie is told, "If I make one exception I'll have to make a thousand", while Josh gets, "If I make an exception for you I have to make an exception for everyone". The music in the Hitchcock, as Charlie finds a newspaper report about the "Merry Widow Murderer" that she now knows to be her uncle, is thunderous and climactic whereas in the Reichardt it is tense and understated, but in both cases the horrified discovery of the truth is followed by an identical camera movement (both characters are even facing in the same direction) which you describe so well as "both slightly contrived and very effective", and as having the result of pinning Josh down. In the earlier film Charlie keeps walking rather than coming to a standstill as Josh does, but there's a watery sensation here too, a kind of underwater feeling that Reichardt picks up on; everything has become very dense around her, it's hard to move and to hear, her sense of moral perspective has just been dealt a shattering blow and the camera's literal distance expresses this, rather than distancing us from it. But given the difference in moral position between Josh and Charlie that I just outlined, the ironies are deliciously plentiful. The connection of the two sequences is so clear that it makes me wonder what further light other aspects of the Hitchcock film might shed on *Night Moves*.

After Josh talks to Harmon he again gets paranoid about a car following him. There's a beautifully abstract shot of two headlights reflected in his rear-view mirror. (Of course the car simply drives past.) This echoes the earlier drive away from the dam; the ensuing sequence is entirely comprised of variations on the morning after the explosion. The next shot looks up again at the sky through the hole in the middle of the yurt roof. Josh lies on his bed, tears in his eyes this time, rather than a smile on his lips. Again he slopes off through the farm. Nobody was watching him in the earlier sequence, whereas here Surprise watches him with concern from the deck outside her own yurt. Unlike in the market, he doesn't see her. This is the claustrophobia of paranoia: he feels that everyone is looking at him, but is insensitive to a situation in which somebody really is. He comes into the main building and sits down just as before. Anne is in the same place she was earlier. But where previously there was a riot of conversation, here there is only a very heavy silence and a refusal of eye contact. Not being looked at is just as bad as being stared at.

We then see Josh at work, the children greeting him as if nothing has happened. Sean calls him over, in yet another variation of figuration that puts Josh in Dena's place, standing in the middle distance in the centre of the frame as she did when he signalled her with his headlights. But whereas the formal echoes I discussed earlier marked out their difference of position, here the point is similarity. Previously Dena was the vulnerable one; it's now Josh's turn.

The film pursues its investigation of speech acts, as Sean tells Josh to make himself scarce without ever saying so. We learn that "Dena and Anne talked, last night" (Harmon was right), although Dena "didn't have to say anything. Anne knows her too well. Anne's

not stupid". The latter two sentences are certainly true but they don't really, or certainly not merely, say what they literally say. When Sean says "I don't know anything, right?", this is pretty close to being literally false. As in his phone conversation with Harmon, Josh is being instructed here, not informed of anything. In his yurt, Josh gathers essential belongings. He drives off in his truck, leaving the right of the frame. From the left, one of the children, in wellies and a blue and black stripy woolly hat, walks into view and then stands watching Josh drive off. A brightly coloured hollow frisbee dangles listlessly in each hand. (There's your motif of circularity again!) It's a great, economical image of a childish state between comprehension and incomprehension, or rather of dawning comprehension. (Which is of course the central theme of *Shadow of a Doubt*.) The child is regretting losing someone who might have played frisbee with them, but in simply standing there and not running or calling after Josh they also express their awareness that there's a world beyond their own interests and that, in this world, Josh's departure might be for the best. Which is a more mature insight than Josh himself seems capable of grasping.

Letter twenty-one

Dear Dom,

So much great stuff in your letter, not least the revelatory citation of Hitchcock in the library scene. Did you make the connection immediately? I've not seen *Shadow of a Doubt* in quite a while but it's always fascinating to me how, and why, such images do or do not or suffer recall or persist in the mind. We've been primed for references to noir and Hitchcock (from Jon Raymond for one) but I admit to being surprised at the shot-for-shot homage, although it's of a wholly different order to the lifts from *Torn Curtain* throughout *The Grand Budapest Hotel*. As you say, the clear echo from film to film surely ties in with important themes, not least the doubling, mirroring, symmetry and splitting that we've been hovering around. We're in a strangely dislocated connective node here, with the shift in "central consciousness" experiencing the shattering blow. The most obvious imperfect reflection comes in regard to the film's structural core of the two Charlies (niece and killer) and how this corresponds to the 'divided cell' of Josh/Dena, which we have again been skirting around. I'm sure you know Truffaut's comment, when in conversation with Hitchcock, that *Shadow of a Doubt* was "systematically built around the figure 'two'" but I couldn't help but smile when looking this up to read how Deleuze, in the first of his *Cinema* books where he cites Truffaut's notion, asserts that in Hitchcock "there is never duel [sic] or double", keen as he is to emphasise *relations* and not lockstep cancellations or unproductive symmetries, I think.[*] But

---

[*] François Truffaut, *Hitchcock (revised Edition)* (Paladin, 1986), p. 293; Gilles Deleuze (trans. Hugh Tomlinson and Barbara Habberjam), *Cinema 1: The Movement-Image* (Continuum, 1985 [2005]), p. 206.

it took me back to the various unstable standoffs we've passed through in *Night Moves*, and I wondered how it might shed another light on the designation of duel or non-duel… and that the key battle, as it were, is the one staged by/in/as/through/with Josh/Dena… Back to the hybrid Raskolnikov that comes to mind when Truffaut (by implication, as he's alluding to films other than *Shadow of a Doubt* too) considers the two Charlies "obviously a single personality split in two".*

Aside from the boldness of cutting to the staring cop in the marketplace scene, there was one other image (a compositional 'flip') that struck me in the sequences you discussed: Josh walks through the parking lot market, away from the camera, a contoured horizon of sun-soaked hills in the background (an odd yellow line bisecting both tarmac and shot—more streak of piss than yellow brick road) < > Josh is on the phone with Harmon, partially obscured behind a foreground line-up of incongruous crystal forms (new age salt licks? Platonic Solid lamps?), which both cut him off and hem him in, adding an elemental, geological emphasis to the potential confinement of "life plus 300 years".

Onward. After the scene in which Josh leaves the farm, we cut to almost complete darkness. The sound of cicadas mixes with a musical accompaniment that could be diegetic—country chords, slide guitar and accordion—a live band at an outdoor gathering. We gradually see Josh's face emerge in close-up as he walks towards the camera, a red tint to the image; a demonic skin tone glow building up? Or another hint of *Apocalypse Now* in chiaroscuro? I'm sure there are countless sequences where faces dip in or out of shadow, but it is so tempting to think of sweaty Kurtz being carved up by the extremes… *are you an assassin* (yet)? Watching

---

* Truffaut, *op. cit.*, p. 293.

Josh emerge here feels deliberate and tentative. It is a different kind of breaking cover, the depth of the shadow indicative of another change in tone. For this is after Josh has been called out, expelled from his settled life. Their secret is out, at least partially, yet there is a sense of potential reset here—new tensions seeding plans—as the extent of the damage is still unknown or as yet deferred. We examine Josh as his discomfort almost twitches, his eyes darting around, unsure and out of practice, not quite knowing what kind of social presence he might have or what reaction he might get. He is thrown by a greeting in the dark, the voice lost in shapeless shadow, yet the anonymous hail suggests he still has currency for now. We watch him negotiate notoriety and anonymity (both immensely isolating) but in a way that is different from earlier sequences – he's *trying* to emerge here it seems, at least tentatively, literally coming out of the dark.

As he keeps walking, the light level increases with the number of people. Just as his isolation seems on the verge of lessening—will he get another foothold or embrace his outlaw-ness?—we cut sharply to a shot of him sitting alone in a ramshackle barn-like space, nursing a drink. It's a self-consciously basic, foundational scene: haybale table in the centre, rustic beams for improvised seating, tethered goat beyond the window. As well as echoing the rustic simple dwellings from *First Cow*, it has the feel of a frontier town at the edge of civilisation, on the eve of wilderness and wandering; you could stage a nativity there. But Reichardt does another smart (and funny) switcheroo here too, as the music wryly switches to an aimless, tentative guitar noodling—perfectly in keeping with the campfire vibes but also (in its slippage into 'amateurism') a terrific rug-pull for Josh's false hope. The stripped back simplicity of the scene also serves to match the constructed (ostensible) simplicity of the ensuing dialogue.

In another section of the barn we see Surprise, wine bottle in hand, as she spots Josh in the corner. This is without being seen by him—a nice continuity with the crisscrossing visibilities you've described so well. Out of sight for a moment, she re-emerges from behind a wall having reset herself, ready to adopt a hint of faux surprise when calling over to Josh. He responds as if woken sharply but is soon returned to his introverted slump by the familiar face. Much of the scene backfills subtext from previous scenes—namely that Surprise is attracted to Josh—whilst thrown off balance by Josh's increasingly desperate state of mind, his paranoiac distance, and proximity to a cliff edge. She is trying to reach him but is not aware how far out he has already drifted.

She's heard he is taking off (supposedly right away but hasn't left yet: an opening) and wonders about a hook up to or in Portland. Josh has plans to head east, but who can say whether or not this is improvised on the spot? The throughline of doubling and alternative paths returns (as well as a wider sense of peril and pressure from the authorities, however unspoken here) as we hear that Corser has been raided by federal agents and had his computers seized. No longer to do with food standards, this raid is now seen as nefarious and potentially spreading: "they're onto something." Surprise says this will a smile, as if both acknowledging her awareness of government overreach but also an understanding of the conspiratorial paranoia of their shared acquaintance—"S'out of this world, right?" Indeed, Josh currently is. His reply is telling in its tacit appeal for guidance: "So what did he do?" *What was Corser's course of action?* In relating that he has cooperated with the authorities (was he raided or did he give them up? What's the agency here?), Surprise ends up making light whilst underscoring the seriousness of Josh's situation. Perhaps this is one of the strategies of having Corser's plight run obliquely alongside in this way, as both an accompaniment and running commentary on the intractability of the law humming in the background.

Surprise is urged to join a group of friends as they pass by, yet her kneejerk affirmative response gets reversed immediately. This is another instance of the language games and performances strewn throughout the film, with more or less conscious play between explicit and implicit meaning. Here it seems heavily layered, folded in with what's at stake (at least for her) in this last conversation before Josh leaves town. She offers the unthinking assent to her friends to Josh, wholly redefined—"God, it's like *go away*, right?"— a gamble of intimacy that may or may not bring them closer: she's not with them, or like them, and this is what she would rather have said. Given that she knows at least something of what's happening, this might be read as a way to get him to confide in her: to connect with him by implying a common distance from people, in being solitary, perhaps even being somewhat like him. It's not convincing. After there is no response, she calculates an escalation, asking Josh if he's talked to Dena. He has his hand to his mouth, perhaps still processing how "these guys" (the Feds) will be looking into *his* situation. When Surprise mentions Sarah, a name that points outside the cast of characters we know in the film, we partially understand Josh's reaction when he seems to both retch and wryly laugh at the fact that Dena is still talking, and more people are involved—a darkly incredulous kind of confirmation bias. From his earlier, desperate (when talking to Harmon) "it only takes one person…", the wheels are now coming off. The flat, shutters-down exchange: "I thought you would know something" "I don't" (itself a call back to statements about knowledge and understanding in the boat) is brutal, as any potential rapport in the conversation has seeped away. Josh smiles and closes off simultaneously, as if some minor point of closure (and release) occurs, one further straw added to the camel's back. Not surprisingly, Surprise takes a swig of wine. She hesitates for a few moments, still sensing there is another way in (great eye movements here) before emphasising her association with Dena as she beats a retreat. But Josh does look up to watch her go (her intuition may have been right) but his gaze hits a potent echo of the marketplace scene. Two men, who were already there when the camera captured passing friends hailing Surprise, are now pointedly staring at Josh. Their faces are isolated by a wooden partition, but the effect is like the threatening presence in the adjacent cell. Background chatter adds to the tagline: just because you're paranoid, it doesn't mean they're not after you. The recurrence of this centripetal paranoia suggests that it has started to take hold and is not going to stop, and perhaps Josh is being pushed to the edges of his right mind.

The next cut jumps to a later stage of the party, with the music (nicely anticipated by the near 'tuning up' feel underneath the previous scenes) erupting into a raucous, gleefully sloppy reel, with drunken dancing by black silhouetted figures crowding the screen. They move both mechanically and maniacally, and we feel we're cutting loose a bit. Beautifully aligned with a chord change, the dark figures part just enough to reveal Josh sitting still and silent in their midst. He is right next to the band (a double bass just visible at top left), as close to the music as possible, yet is cut off from the bawdy, Hogarthian absurdity of the revels. The

cinematography is great here, with Josh highlighted in a depth-of-field island, black figures both in front of him and behind. He is obscured and cut off again. We're in metaphor land again, with something that edges ever closer to horror: Josh plagued by demons, on the verge of madness and self-pity (every other presence a blank non-entity). Potential references abound here (not least to the silhouetted worker from the feed store) and range from Goya's *The Sleep of Reason Produces Monsters* (1799), the danse macabre of *The Seventh Seal*, to iPod adverts from the 2000s. It is also quite theatrical and stage-y, as if these were shadow puppets choreographed as all-too-present figures that are also indistinguishable from the surroundings. In fact, I was most strongly reminded of the shadows in *Ghost* (1990), the sounds of which still manage to strike a nerve somewhere down my spine. As well as having the sense that he is at risk of being swallowed and erased, Josh's stillness here also suggests he is caught in a kind of limbo, caught as much as the child watching him leave a few scenes ago, between comprehension and incomprehension, setting up the fateful scenes to come.

Letter twenty-two

Dear David,

I don't think I've ever made the connection with *Shadow of a Doubt* while watching *Night Moves*, but it came to mind immediately on reading your description of Reichardt's crane shot in the library. I was pretty astonished at how direct and unmistakable the allusion is. (The whole question of allusions in her films is worthy of further exploration. I just rewatched *The Mastermind* and there is a clear evocation of *It Happened One Night*—bus trips combined with hitch-hiking—as well as a circling pan that echoes Antonioni's *The Passenger* as directly as the crane shot evokes Hitchcock. But in none of these cases does it seem like we're dealing with anything as crude as a key to the film.) I'm finding it hard to work out precisely what we're supposed to do with the allusion here, unless— as I suggested—it's the corrosive effect of doubt that is most relevant. I'm not buying the idea of Josh and Dena as doubles, somehow; too many of the film's achievements seem predicated on the idea of Josh as its central consciousness, even if this isn't something we know right from the beginning of the film. That remark of Deleuze's is interesting, though; his film writings can always prompt interesting reflections, even if (having come out the other side of co-editing a collection on the *Cinema* books) I'm increasingly uncomfortable with the extent to which the desire to say something interesting trumps careful attention to the films themselves. Clearly "never duel or double" is hyperbole. I think going back to the French helps a bit, as it often does given the shortcomings of the translation. (Did I ever mention my favourite Deleuze translation fact, which is that Hugh Tomlinson, one of the two translators of the *Cinema* books, is a KC whose cases have included leading Rebekah Vardy's team in the "Wagatha Christie" case?). What is rendered as "both appeal to the same state of the world" is "prennent à témoin un même état du monde".* I think "prendre à témoin" is something like "call to witness" or, perhaps more idiomatically, "call to testify". So the point is, I take it, that the two Charlies aren't just adversaries or mirror images but that they see the world in the same way. I'm not sure about the coherence of what Deleuze goes on to say—if the state of the world declares to one person that they are justified in murder and to another the very opposite, wouldn't we normally say that they don't at all see the world in the same way? But he's definitely on to something in the sense that the two characters are connected more than they are simple inversions of one another.

Robert Pippin's chapter on *Shadow of a Doubt* in *Filmed Thought* is excellent on this, and on how unsettling it is for our view of morality—and all the more so because of how easy it is to miss, how readily we can take the young Charlie as straightforwardly good.† (Pippin points out the readiness with which she tries to get her uncle to leave town, with not a thought given— by either character or, most likely, audience—to the fact that this would no doubt lead to more murder, elsewhere.) Hence all the references to telepathy in the film, which is also connected to sexual deviance. (My favourite joke about this is the unmistakable evocation of a tone of sexual disgust we hear in the post office mistress's response to young Charlie's questioning her about telepathy, which she mishears as "telegraphy": "I only send telegrams the *normal* way.") There's no hint

---

* Deleuze, *op. cit.*, p. 206 and Gilles Deleuze, *Cinéma 1: L'Image-mouvement* (Les Éditions de Minuit, 1983), p. 272.
† Robert B. Pippin, "Confounding Morality in Alfred Hitchcock's *Shadow of a Doubt*", in *Filmed Thought: Cinema as Reflective Form* (University of Chicago Press, 2020), pp. 67-95.

of telepathy between Josh and Dena, which perhaps is what dooms her. In ways that resonate with Cavell's studies of scepticism in cinema, it's almost as if only a telepathic connection could reassure Josh about her intentions. Which means that only her death could reassure him. I love your phrase "common distance"; we could see the film as an exploration of the common distance between all of us. There is something metaphysical in what Josh is trying to achieve in killing her: I don't think I had quite appreciated on previous viewings the pointlessness of the murder, given that Dena has already told Anne what they did, even if not in so many words. What's so powerful about the ending is the way the world collapses in around Josh so that this distance is all the room for manoeuvre he has left.

Which is to anticipate doubly. Yes, Josh kills Dena. Is this something we are led to expect? Clearly, the possibility is evoked, but that is not the same thing. Do the film's connections to genre make her death *more* or *less* likely? I suppose the answer must be *more*, given that this has now clearly become a "heist gone wrong" movie. But an achievement of this film is the way it somehow holds in suspension the relationship between Josh's paranoia and the threat that the authorities now represent to his freedom. As you say, invoking the great Pynchonian theme, just because you're paranoid doesn't mean they're not after you. They very much *are* after him, and yet the texture of the film makes his *personality* (his impatience, his self-pity, his introspectiveness) seem to be what is driving his actions, more than his—on one level perfectly rational—terror of discovery and imprisonment. And yet the film's realism (for want of a better word) holds this is check very effectively, I think. "Is this really the kind of film in which people murder each other in cold blood?" is a relevant question, and—for me at least—my initial experience of it led to the answer "no". I suppose I'm saying that in presenting the murder the film isn't merely negotiating issues of plausibility, but almost a second-order effect: the plausibility of plausibility, which we can only assess relative to our understanding of the *kind* of film we're watching. (All this might seem far too intellectual, but I think this is very much the sort of thing one can *feel* while watching a film.) And the complexity here must have something to do with the way the film disappointed so many viewers; they could only see it as something going wrong, as expectations having been disappointed, rather than those expectations being part of the film's very material.

We also need to ask whether *Josh* expected to kill Dena. I think it is very clear that he didn't plan to. (Not the same thing. Had the thought crossed his mind?) The next shot after the sequence you discussed shows the spa at night, obviously from Josh's point of view across the street. A woman cycles away, calling "good night!". The next shot shows Dena and a woman leaving the spa, the woman pushing a bike. (Which makes things a little confusing, since this suggests that the two women with bikes are one and the same, which they aren't. Normally I'd say something like "but it adds to the overall sense of disorientation", but I think the two bikes are actually just confusing, to no real purpose.) Clearly Dena has allowed these women in after hours: "Hope you don't get in trouble for this", the woman tells her. Dena says she won't. (Obvious irony: opening late pales into insignificance compared to what she may very well get into very deep "trouble" for.) They discuss her rash, which Dena says happens "whenever I'm stressed". The whole sequence is a very effective study in the close-up and in point of view. The next few shots evoke horror film syntax. Dena returns inside, locks the gate, then enters the main building. We see, from her point of view, the front door standing ajar. A new age-y wooden flute on the soundtrack is both plausible for the surroundings and effectively grating. Dena locks the front door and puts the key away in the draw of the cash register. There's a great shot of her reflected in the window to the right of frame, almost as if she is simultaneously outside and inside.

There follows a shot of Dena putting the key away, surrounded by darkness, the camera swaying slightly. Then a close-up of the key going into a drawer next to cash, cheques and other odds and ends. Dena pulls out a blue crystal and looks at it, holding it up to the light as it spins on its string. It refracts blue light onto her face, and then—slightly unrealistically—onto Josh's, in extreme close-up. The light reveals that they are in the same space together; perhaps it has other metaphoric resonances as well, although they aren't entirely clear to me. The crystal belongs to the same new age-y register as the flute; possibly its light represents a kind of healing Dena would like to invoke (but can't really bring herself to believe in?) and that Josh definitely rejects. The more distant shot of Dena is repeated and it becomes clear, if it wasn't before, that he's looking at her from inside a cupboard or wardrobe, like Jeffrey in *Blue Velvet*, but without the sexual charge. The earlier shot from across the street, despite its slightly disorientating qualities, becomes very important in balancing our perspective of the two characters here. Without it, we would be wondering if Josh is going to turn up. With it, and with the open door, we surely know that he's here. Despite what I said earlier about Josh being the central consciousness of the film, in this particular sequence the balance between the two of them is very adroitly handled indeed. Our position is expertly suspended between that of the threatened and the threatening. (This puts me in mind of another Hitchcock film, although there the effect is achieved by different means: *Strangers on a Train*.)

An extreme close-up of Dena lets us see the rash on her neck in great detail. She turns round and suddenly Josh is there, motionlessly staring at her. He finds it hard to answer her question, "What are you doing here?", his throat working without any words coming out. She approaches gingerly, clearly frightened, and tells him to go home, at which he pushes her back and says that he "just wanted to make sure that you're OK". He says that he's been "not so good, and if I'm not good, and you're not good…" He leaves the conclusion of the syllogism unspoken. The lack of telepathy: it's not that he knows what she's feeling because of what he's feeling, it's that he has evidence of how she's feeling—the rash, for example—and is drawing conclusions from it: "I just think it's important that we know what we feel". Then she suddenly hits him over the head with some kind of soft rattle, and they struggle. He tells her to stay off the phone and the computer, to get out of town if she has to. She knees him in the stomach and he collapses, then grabs her foot as she tries to run away. She falls over, they struggle briefly, and she manages to kick him hard in the face, get up and run out of the building. As Josh drags himself up he looks after her with a hard expression and the flute is joined by electronic music similar to that which we heard during the explosive-laying sequence at the dam. Would it be crude to say that this is the moment he decides to kill her?

Josh follows Dena, limping slightly. The camera gives us his literal point of view and the flute disappears from the soundtrack, leaving only trickling water and the electronic score. Eventually he enters the sauna, steeling himself before opening the door. It's all orange light and steam, in an excellently plausible use of images verging on abstraction. She leaps out at him, snarling, and he strangles her, which is shown mostly through extreme close-ups of the two of them, her eyes widening, until her death is represented in metonymic fashion through her struggling feet gradually becoming still. Josh's close-up reminds me of one of Justin Theroux's distorted face as he has sex with Laura Dern in Lynch's *INLAND EMPIRE*. I suppose there must be sexual connotations here (she on her back, he above, both of them grunting), but the film handles them delicately; they don't overpower the mise-en-scène. Interestingly, Reichardt has suggested that she mismanaged the use of close-ups in the film: "Okay, for instance, when I was watching *Night Moves*, I was looking at the first shots of Jesse Eisenberg. With the combination of what I'm doing and what he's doing, I give his whole thing away in the first ten seconds.… Poor Jesse, I have all of these close-ups of him at the beginning of the film—that should happen way, way later."* I don't think she's right about this. I think it's important that the close-ups in the latter parts of the film don't seem like revelations, that the film destabilizes the connection between the close-up and the candid. We don't necessarily see the most when we can see the most clearly.

It's important to note how the first genuine violence in this sequence comes from Dena. Josh pushes and grabs her, but not with any real violence. She didn't know what she was grabbing, and could easily have knocked him out, or at least done his head some real damage, had something more solid come to hand. Then there is the knee, the kick, and the leap. I think this is very delicately handled. The film doesn't for a moment suggest that she brings on her own murder, but it does show how things play out in such a way that Josh could at least attempt to tell himself that he reacted more than he acted. This is possibly what he's attempting during the subsequent long take of him behind the wheel of his truck, teary-eyed. Who, and what, is he sorry for, and about?

---

* https://mubi.com/en/notebook/posts/the-owl-and-the-cow-a-conversation-with-kelly-reichardt.

Letter twenty-three

Dear Dom,

One wonders if such a clear reference to Hitchcock was nonetheless intended to stay buried in the film, less a key to interpretation than a secreted homage, a wink to both filmmaker and genre. Weirdly, while starting to think about this again, I was reading a passage from Anton Ehrenzweig (quoted in David Toop's book on Dr John's *Gris-gris*!) which describes Wagner's use of quiet instrumental leitmotifs that inevitably get submerged in his overall wall of sound. Although such insertions might initially suggest a kind of "pedantic allusion to a dramatic idea which is only discovered by reading the score", Ehrenzweig maintains that they nonetheless impart a "decisive difference [on the] final beauty of sound and the plastic quality of an expanding musical space".* This quality connects with what you call the texture of the film, I think. Although echoing the library scene from *Shadow of a Doubt* might not unlock anything, I like to think it could infuse the film with a latent genre memory (as it were)—an engram, even an imprint of Hitchcock himself. As if this kind of inheritance could not only contribute to the film's dramatic shape but also the sense of baked-in genre expectation: the water already flavoured by the leaves. Amidst the perversely comedic set-up of the murder in the New Age spa, there's something purposefully noirish and Hitchcockian about the site of the sauna for the murder too—as close to another homage without repeating a shower stabbing—another play with the aggregate states of water as a barometer /

---

* Anton Ehrenzweig, *The Hidden Order of Art: A Study in the Psychology of Artistic Imagination*, pp. 91-92; quoted in David Toop, *Two-headed Doctor: Listening for Ghosts in Dr. John's Gris-Gris* (Strange Attractor Press, 2024), p. 70.

trigger of Josh's inner turbulence, arguably reinforced by him seeking out the valve of the slow-moving river in the immediate aftermath. I really like what you write about the plausibility of plausibility in relation to how *Night Moves* keeps things suspended, almost through doublespeak, which makes me realise how strange a film it is. In a sense the murder is reversed by what surrounds it—as you say, it seems both anomalous and inevitable—not breaking the fourth wall or anything but overtly pushing at its believability. It also has an interesting relation to Reichardt's interest in the stalled agency of marginal characters who are often limited by structural conditions (be they economic, social, environmental, etc.) whereas here Josh is forced (obliged? permitted?) into committing the murder by the conventions of genre. This is a thriller; in generic terms, his agency is jumpstarted; he almost *has* to kill her. In her handling of humour, if nothing else, Reichardt does not endorse this logic so much as expose it. The genre imprint is there, but more often than not is undercut or worn on the sleeve.

A sense of substructure seems relevant when considering the connection between Josh and Dena. The two of them being doubles or inversions doesn't work, you're right, yet there is something pointed in the nature of their *split* and the starkly different paths they take: each informed by and entangled with the presence of the other. From what might be thought of as 'common conditions'—shared political conviction, shared preparation, shared risk—and apparent solidarity, they end up as fatal adversaries. In this respect, my understanding of Deleuze's comment on the two Charlies in *Shadow of a Doubt* was not that the characters see the world in the same way but that the same conditions of the world produce (and justify) their contrasting attitudes. They are both symptoms and products of the same state of things. With Josh and Dena, the film initially suggests they indeed see the world in broadly similar terms yet devolve into violently antithetical positions through the consequences of collective action. People reacting differently to the same events might seem unremarkable, but *Night Moves* seems to foreground it as something structurally (politically, philosophically) significant, and to shadow its structure. And if what engenders the common only feeds what is peculiarly violent in private individualism, does this imply a metaphysical question as to where, precisely, the split occurs? Is this also what we've been looking for in hinges and the like?

Reichardt delicately charts the disintegration of (ostensible) unity to suggest that it was unsustainable, or flawed, from the outset. This retrospectively casts earlier depictions of Josh and Dena's togetherness in an ambiguous light. They are not clearly presented as a couple, though they could have been lovers; there are hints of concern, jealousy, and irritation, yet things are always held at a distance. What binds them most securely is not intimacy but purpose. Their plan functions as the mechanism of alignment, temporarily bridging emotional and ideological gaps. Once that mechanism fails (or doesn't hold to expectations), other, previously latent differences are released and the film becomes almost entirely about how that divergence ultimately leads to disastrous collision. Gendered archetypes begin to matter here, not as rigid determinisms but as patterned responses (rash vs hallucination). Arguably, the film suggests that the male character's paranoid need for control alienates and ultimately betrays any sense of collective ecological liberation they claimed to seek. Josh's narcissism redirects the imperative for action on ecological collapse away from critique of systems toward self-interest and violence—the very motors of the system he decries. It is worth remembering that all the threats Josh perceives—capture, imprisonment, being wrong—also apply to Dena. What differs is how those threats are metabolised.

Of course, there's also the odd problem of Harmon's role in any notion of splitting and binary connections (however uneven). If you might forgive my flights of fancy, one might risk further crudity by considering a triangulation of psychological terms: Josh aligned with the id, his violence impulsive and poorly thought through; Harmon's disembodied, rationalising voice (*Something's gotta happen, man!...* if there's telepathy going on, is it in this running commentary?) functioning as ego; and Dena increasingly occupying the position of superego, oriented toward guilt, shame, and moral reckoning. This is more than a stretch, of course, not least in how it risks Pippin's wrath for positioning Dena as moral authority incarnate (when we know it's not so simple)... perhaps better to ponder how Dena becomes the site onto which Josh pointlessly displaces his own guilt. As such, the murder is an attempt to silence conscience, snuff out self-doubt, to reject moral and legal constraint: to free the 'outlaw'. Just as some old Freudian might point out that a functioning psyche requires all three agencies, after all, the result is not liberation but collapse.

By the way, in terms of "metaphoric resonances" with the blue crystal in the cash register (as well as the other spiral and circular motifs), it might be that they are remnants from Abbey's novel, however the details get mashed up or which characters they are applied to. Describing the home of Abbzug, the only female member of the Monkey Wrench Gang, Abbey writes that the "interior of [the] dome glittered like the heart of a geode, with dangling silvery mobiles and electric lanterns made of multiperforated No.8 tin cans hanging from the ceiling, and crystalline clusters of mirrors and baubles attached at random to the curved interior".* He offers it as a nod to simple pleasures, perhaps for our purposes a glow of a life beyond very present troubles.

So, after the murder, Josh is on the road again and it is made clear that he travels some distance through the night. The switch to a shot of an early hour highway is starkly beautiful and portentous, the central vanishing point adding a sense of inevitability, along-side the apocalyptic feel of the pylon-gallows lining the road, reminiscent of Brueghel or Bosch. We hear Josh explaining that he visited Dena last night, yet it is only after he has claimed an 'accident' has happened that we cut to him sat behind the wheel in a retail park, a seemingly random location chosen at the behest of low fuel or exhaustion. From his response we hear Harmon catching on immediately and veering the conversation away from specifics, prompting Josh by rhetorically asking whether or not Dena "quit on us". This offers Josh another layer of distancing and rationalisation: a euphemistic use of language (is it macho? sporty?

---

* *The Monkey Wrench Gang*, p. 41.

vaguely militaristic?) that he didn't expect but which he instantly adopts. A development from what you point out about Josh being able to say he reacted more than acted. The one-sided phone call again contrasts Josh's tearful tension with Harmon's calm, clinical self-preservation. We see Josh's hands squeezing and picking at the steering wheel, yet hear them both fall in with the cynical misogyny of blaming Dena for her own death, as if she were not man enough to stay 'on the team'. Threatened for a while, whatever camaraderie there was has now collapsed into gendered contempt. Yet even here there is a whiff of black humour in Josh's near-whispered "she quit by accident", a line that carries a near-slapstick absurdity (akin to Dena reaching for the rainstick in the earlier confrontation) but again not played for laughs outright. Given an 'out' by this voice, Josh appeals for more. Now strangely laden with "a lot of stuff", he wants company, to go somewhere quiet and off-grid with Harmon. This avenue closes too, as Harmon fobs him off with instructions: "You gotta get real lost now. You gotta get real lost and stay lost." Josh's misanthropic, loner tendency arguably needs to become something else. But the phraseology is rich here, as if containing a new age-y maxim to the effect that getting 'real lost' might actually lead to finding oneself. But, of course, the hollowing out of such idioms has been staged throughout the film. It's obvious to say that Josh is already lost, yet Harmon's summative "that's it" is brutal in its meld of simplicity and seeming irreversibility. It adds a certain hopelessness to proceedings. Josh knows this enough to assent as Harmon rings off, a firm tear tracking down his cheek. He is shellshocked, lost in thought… now what? The phone switches hands.

The next few shots — alternating between close-ups of Josh's face and what he sees from the truck —

I find intriguing. He watches a young man in a hoodie walk from a parked car to a grocery outlet as another bland sedan creeps past. His expression changes. Then another, older man wearing a hat walks toward the same store. Josh's demeanour, at least to my mind, hardens each time, as if he not only realises that, in this moment at least, these people are *not looking for him*, and that he *hasn't yet been caught*, but there's also a distinct sense that he holds these anonymous figures in contempt. (I wonder if this connects to what Reichardt means in terms of giving "his whole thing away"— a comment that confuses me slightly—perhaps linking his gaze with his capacity to murder?) Again, we watch Josh plot out a next move, curtailed, as you say, by his lack of room for manoeuvre. He breaks open his mobile, pulls the sim card out from beneath the battery, then emerges from the truck. He deposits the phone body into the back of a nearby pickup, then slots the sim into the boot crack of an adjacent saloon. One cannot help but see this as another split, a division of his 'signal' such that it bifurcates away from the still point where he remains. He walks slowly, slouched and wary (as if dispersing tunnel soil in a prison yard...) toward another store that we haven't seen before. A small red sign reading HELP WANTED sits in the window, small enough to miss, and it is not clear if Josh sees this as he enters or beforehand. It is clearly another telling plant, another pointing arrow or caption to the action, this time reminding me of the potent non-closure of THIS IS NOT AN EXIT ending Bret Easton Ellis' *American Psycho*, rendered as a brass sign in Mary Harron's film adaptation.

There's something compelling here in not knowing the extent to which Josh is comfortable with improvising now, or how aware he is of what he's doing. He walks into the Big 5 Sporting Goods outlet and the ambience changes around him. Anodyne rock guitar accompanies a sliding pan across rows of binoculars and folding knives. The conveyor belt motion of the camera offers a parade of commodities like the Generation Game. We jump to another muffled pop song (Sun Rai's 2012 song "San Francisco Street"; a loungey road tune whose accompanying video of nighttime freeways echoes sequences in *Night Moves*, and which includes the mocking refrain 'it's all in front of you') playing over a glide past blank-faced mannequins posed at a freezing barbecue. It recalls numerous family groups we've encountered before, now turned into ciphers. We're back in a commodified fantasy of the outdoors. And Josh being surrounded by the accoutrements of camping after having inadvertently killed a camper marks a dark irony. A singular penitence it is to live close to your sin...

Another shot sees Josh standing in front of a wall of sleeping bags, looking for all the world like some Bartleby-like figure, starting to blank out. He notices and zips up the exposed innards of one sleeping bag (a nod to the gore we didn't get?), almost the late confirmation of a pathological need for control. Were it not for a continuity jump, we might think he had lost himself in this faux-browsing reverie (how long is he here?) but he is suddenly elsewhere in the store when offered the very help he needs, notably by a female shop assistant not dissimilar in age and look to Dena. He rejects it out of habit before catching himself and quickly asking about the advertised job. The assistant watches him warily as he follows a supervisor to the front desk. In some ways, this is a strange moment—he has just murdered someone and his first act is to apply for a job? But it is a practical move, to establish a new foothold with his fake ID. One might wonder about metaphors throughout the film of the herd vs. the individual (outlaw), and perhaps one way to get 'real lost' in Josh's mind is to fill in the form, get a regular job, to disappear into anonymous conformity. There is to be no wild final confrontation, no Bolivian bum-rush at San Vicente, no suicide-by-cop. This is the ideologue's worst nightmare, it seems. With nowhere to go, you must become what you despise to survive. But the pen hovers over the form, shaking in his hand. He cannot do it. Josh looks up and sees what is the final shot of the film, an image of a circular convex mirror, filling the right half of the screen, angled downward from a supporting column. It contains two people, a man and a woman, amid the shelves and racks of goods, sharing the same 'bubble' but clearly disengaged from one another and their surroundings. Both are pinned to what David Lynch might spittingly call their "fucking telephone", jacked into where they aren't, one balancing a disposable cup (emphasising the nested circles of the composition) whilst tapping away at the screen, the other conducting a call whilst fingering a circular rack of jackets. Even amidst the placeless excess of the shop floor, buoyed by commodities, these folks are elsewhere, sucked in by other virtual storehouses of consumption and distraction. The shot also ties in with the film's persistent theme of surveillance—whether it be the systems the trio try to avoid being detected by or Josh watching from trucks and cupboards, from an impenetrable skull. The film ends in this puddle of alienation, having disintegrated from shared, idealistic actions of solidarity and resistance to profoundly anxious images of destructive isolation.

When we cut to the credits, with no obvious closure or catharsis to come with it, my feeling was that we are left much as Josh is left, looking into the mirror and being strangely contained and thrown by it. In the interview cited previously, Jon Raymond talked about wanting sufficient closure in this 'non-ending' of having Josh enter a place of punishment, even a "kind of purgatory".* No doubt this comment relates more to the term's everyday sense of being suspended between undecidable outcomes than any doctrinal sense of the saved being purified before entering the kingdom of Heaven. In any case, what terrace of Mount Purgatory would Josh be on anyway? Could his suspension contain any possibility of redemption?

---

* Sorrento, *op. cit.*, p. 124.

On special offer? Would he feel any urge to accept his suffering as an initiation into a new, unknown life of grace? I'd say that *Night Moves* offer a satirical punch-line that suggests that when such narcissistic absolutism (nurtured by unfettered capitalism) is baked into radical activism it only leads to its reinforcement. Everything gets swallowed up into stock. Our outlaw is given nowhere to go and he gets trapped inside, between conviction and consequence, unable to move.

Letter twenty-four

Dear David,

Part of me doesn't want to say anything more. You've brought us to the end of the film so elegantly that a clean break seems preferable to any lingering. But then you did have the first word, so perhaps I should avail myself of the last. (Last purely in literal terms of course; I don't want to make any pretentions to conclusiveness!)

The ending of the film is so quiet and yet so shattering, and it ties in so many things without any sense of contrivance. One of which I'd managed somehow not really to register in previous viewings — namely the connection that you point out between the camping gear and the fact that the man who died was a camper. (If we were to extend your psychoanalytic reading we might be able to use that to say more about Josh.) And yet, despite the genuine desolation, the ending somehow manages to be quite funny as well, the stance of relaxed authority taken up by the manager who is significantly younger than Josh being one example.

However, while not exactly disagreeing with your interpretation, I do want to suggest a slightly different take. Your description of Josh as trapped between (or perhaps paralysed by) "conviction and consequence" is terrific, but I think it's quite important to register that the fact that he can't fill out the form is not, or certainly not exclusively, psychological. It's more or less literally true that, as you put it, "he cannot do it". What exactly is he going to write? Although it seems superficially similar, my feeling is that this isn't at all the kind of ambiguous ending that hovers between different ways that the story might play out. This is the end.

While I don't for a minute dispute the characterisation of the film's final shot as an "anxious image of destructive isolation", I think it's a huge achievement of the film that it's also perfectly banal, and not in any aggressive sense. It's just a couple of people in a shop on their phones, under neon lighting, living ordinary lives—something Josh will no longer be able to do. And so, while there is satire in the ending, I don't quite want to say that the film as whole ends on a satirical note. The notion that "when such narcissistic absolutism (nurtured by unfettered capitalism) is baked into radical activism it only leads to its reinforcement" might make the film seem moralistic in a way that I think it takes pains to avoid. Josh deserves what he gets, but the film neither exults in nor bemoans this; it doesn't temper things because we like him or "identify" with him, or by reminding us of the nobility of the cause and so suggesting it was just the way he went about things that was at fault. Cavell writes at the end of *The World Viewed* about the way that film "registers absolute isolation".* What I love about the ending of *Night Moves* is that it finds an utterly original way of doing so.

---

* *The World Viewed*, p. 159.

Sticking Place Books (stickingplacebooks.com) is a New York-based publisher specializing in cinema, offering interview books, memoirs, critical and historical studies, screenplays, and essay collections. Our titles include:

Lessons with Kiarostami, edited by Paul Cronin

In the Shadow of Trees: The Collected Poetry of Abbas Kiarostami

Still Film Crazy (After All These Years) by Patrick McGilligan

It's Only a Movie by Bruce Joel Rubin

Three Visionary Screenplays by Bruce Joel Rubin

Playing Among the Stars: Conversations with Damien Chazelle by Nathan Réra

The Magic Eye: The Cinema of Stanley Kubrick by Neil Hornick

A Shared Cinema: Conversations with Michael Ciment by N. T. Bihn

The Naughty Bits: What the Censors Wouldn't Let You See in Hollywood's Most Famous Movies by Nat Segaloff

Mexico: The Aztec Account of the Conquest by Werner Herzog

My Lunches with Henry Jaglom by Daniel Kremer

Bender's L.A. by Michael Elias

My Strange Love: Selected Film Reviews and Essays, 2001–2021 by Stuart Klawans

Dentists with Guns by David Mamet

Late Style in Film by Collin Brinkmann

Dressing the Story by Debra McGuire

Metafiction by David LaRocca

The Most Important Art by Ian Christie

Two Screenplays by Eve Babitz and Michael Elias

All That Black by Cristiana Astori

Night Moves: Twenty-four letters
by Dominic Lash and David R J Stent

Body Parts & Zero Tolerance
by Alex Cox and Rudy Wurlitzer

www.ingramcontent.com/pod-product-compliance
Lightning Source LLC
Chambersburg PA
CBHW070903160726
48004CB00003B/1221